THE REALM OF MATTER

Thou hast ordered all things in number
and measure and weight.
—*Wisdom of Solomon.*

Nil natum est in corpore ut uti
Possemus, sed quod natum est, id procreat
usum.

Nothing has arisen in the body in order
that we may use it, but when anything has
arisen it creates its use.—Lucretius.

Καὶ γὰρ εἰ αὐτὴ ἡ ψυχὴ τῇ ὕλῃ ἐγέννησε
παθοῦσα, καὶ εἰ ἐκοινώνησεν αὐτῇ καὶ ἐγένετο
κακή, ἡ ὕλη αἰτία παροῦσα· οὐ γὰρ ἂν ἐγένετο
εἰς αὐτὴν μὴ τῇ παρουσίᾳ αὐτῆς τὴν γένεσιν
λαβοῦσα.—For if the (heavenly) soul, having
become subservient to matter, passed into
process, and if by communion with matter
she was corrupted, extant matter by its
presence was the cause thereof; for the
(heavenly) soul would not pass into matter,
if matter was not at hand to lend her a
changeful existence.—Plotinus.

THE

REALM OF MATTER

BOOK SECOND

OF

REALMS OF BEING

BY

GEORGE SANTAYANA

NEW YORK

CHARLES SCRIBNER'S SONS

1930

G

First Published 1930

PRINTED IN GREAT BRITAIN
BY R. & R. CLARK, LIMITED, EDINBURGH

PREFACE

THERE is a prejudice in some quarters against the word
Matter, even where the thing and all its uses are most
honoured. Matter seems an evil to the sour moralist
because it is often untoward, and an occasion of im-
perfection or conflict in things. But if he took a wider
view matter would seem a good to him, because it is
the principle of existence: it is all things in their
potentiality, and therefore the condition of all their
excellence or possible perfection. In metaphysics,
however, the objection to matter is not that matter is
evil, but that it is superfluous, unknowable, or even
non-existent; and I might easily have avoided certain
antagonisms by giving to matter a more fashionable
name and speaking instead of the realm of events or of
space-time or of evolution. I might even have taken
refuge in that half-poetical language to which I am
not disinclined, and might have called the realm of
matter simply nature. But nature, events, space-
time, and even evolution (when this means simply
metamorphosis) are indicative terms, containing no
ontological analysis: my problem is precisely to distinguish in this vast flood of existence the planes and
qualities of reality which it contains or presupposes.
I wish to note the differences and the relations between

the animate and the inanimate, the physical and the
moral, the psychological and the logical, the temporal
and the eternal.   It is very true that one and the same
flux of events exemplifies now one and now another
of these realms of being, or variously impinges upon
them; but this amphibious character of existence is far
from being a reason for not distinguishing those realms.
On the contrary, besides the inherent differences in
them which nothing can ever obliterate, there is an
added reason why the naturalist should discriminate
them. He is not merely living, like the animals, but
professing to describe the world; and the sense of
existence would remain a merely emotional burden,
and life a blind career, unless he began by discriminat-
ing the essences which it discloses, in their hetero-
geneity, hierarchy, and succession.

If, then, in turning to the study of existence I had
avoided the word matter, there would have been a
sort of treason in that subterfuge. I do not mean
treason so much to matter itself, because the intrinsic
essence of matter being unknown, it may be figured
almost indifferently by any image of sense or thought,
as by " the gods " or " the devil ", provided that expectation and action are not misled by that symbol.
I mean rather treason to spirit, to truth, to essence, to
those trembling immaterial lights and that infinite
immutable background which, unless sharply contrasted with the matter which they surround, may be
transposed in confused apprehension to the plane of
matter, and saddled with material functions. Have
not both truth and spirit, not to speak of essence, been
represented in our day as things physical, temporal,
instrumental, and practical? Ontologically, this attitude

is absurd, and a mere failure in discernment; but
taken apostolically—for it is zealously espoused—it
expresses a genuine and perfectly legitimate allegiance:
that respect for matter only, which characterises the
psyche when absorbed in action and in circumstances.
Life marks a mechanical complication, maintained in a
world where it did not always exist; and the psyche,
in her fundamental impulse, is perfectly content that
all her ardent labour should end in a vain redistribution of matter, or should never end. It would seem
idle from her point of view, and rather mad, that any
spirit should ever disengage itself from that process and
should come to find in it some satisfying essence, so
that in discerning and possessing this essence it might
transcend that remorseless flux and might look away
from it to an eternal world. In the reversion of
philosophy (which in spite of itself is a form of spirit)
to exclusive sympathy with the flux of matter, there is
accordingly a too domestic virtue or exaggerated piety,
like that of a fair daughter devoting her whole existence
to nursing her old mother. Free spirit lets the dead
bury their dead, and takes no thought for the morrow;
and it redeems the labouring world by bringing joy
into it.

Theoretical scruples about the reality of matter are
of two sorts: they may be sceptical and empirical,
based on the fact that matter is no immediate datum
of intuition; or they may be scientific and logical,
based on the suspicion that some particular idea of
matter may be unfit or inadequate to express its true
nature. These two kinds of objection are mutually
contradictory; for the one condemns matter for not
being a human sensation, and the other condemns

matter for being only a human idea. The first objection involves a retreat to the subjective sphere; and however legitimate such a retreat may be in romantic soliloquy, it is in principle destructive of all science or even belief. The postulate of substance—the assumption that there are things and events prior to the discovery of them and independent of this discovery—underlies all natural knowledge. The refinements which may supervene on this conviction ought never to shake it, and do not do so when they are fruitful. Therefore the first sort of objection against matter—that it is a thing-in-itself antecedent to human experience—may be dismissed at once as vain and sophistical; for it rescinds that animal faith, or that common sense, which is the beginning of art and of science and their perpetual presupposition.

There remains the second difficulty: the suspicion, or the clear perception, that some special description of matter—say that of Democritus or that of Descartes —is inadequate or mistaken. But of course all human notions of matter, even if not positively fabulous, must be wholly inadequate; otherwise the natural philosopher would be claiming a plenitude of miraculous illumination such as no prophet ever thought to possess. Human ideas of matter are initially as various as human contacts with it, and as human sensations in its presence. These ideas are sensuous and pictorial from the beginning. They are then variously sifted and refined according to people's progress in the arts of comparison and calculation. In popular speech the word matter continues to suggest the popular aspects of natural things; in scientific speech, at each stage of it, the word comes to denote such aspects of those same

things as have become calculable at that stage. Thus to
a stone-cutter extension and impenetrability may well
seem the essence of matter; the builder, intent on the
strains and dangers of position, will add degrees of
cohesion and weight to his definition. At this stage
metaphysicians and moralists will look down on matter
as something gross and dead, and will imagine that
motion and organisation must be imposed on matter
from without: not seeing that this external force, if it
governed and moved matter, would be the soul of
matter, and much nearer to its proper essence than
the æsthetic aspects which its aggregates may wear to
the human eye. Yet what could be more obviously
material than thunder and lightning, sunshine and rain,
from which the father of the gods borrowed his poetic
substance? Weight and figure are not more characteristic of matter than are explosiveness, swiftness, fertility,
and radiation. Planters and breeders of animals, or
poets watching the passing generations of mankind,
will feel that the heart and mystery of matter lie in
the seeds of things, *semina rerum*, and in the customary
cycles of their transformation. It is by its motion and
energy, by its fidelity to measure and law, that matter
has become the substance of our world, and the
principle of life and of death in it. The earliest sages,
no less than the latest moderns, identified matter with
fire, æther, or fluids, rather than with stocks and
stones; the latter are but temporary concretions, and
always in the act of growing or crumbling. Even those
who, partly for dialectical reasons, reduced matter to
impenetrable atoms, attributed all its fertility to the
play of collisions which swept perpetually through the
void and drove those dead atoms into constellations

and vortices and organisms. This endless propulsion and these fated complications were no less material, and far more terrible, than any monumental heap into which matter might sometimes be gathered, and which to a gaping mind might seem more substantial. If any poet ever felt the life of nature in its truth, irrepressible, many-sided, here flaming up savagely, there helplessly dying down, that poet was Lucretius, whose materialism was unqualified.

Finally, in our own times, when physics speculates chiefly on bodies so remote or minute as to be known only through variations in light, matter seems to evaporate into these visible variations, as if light had no source, or as if man had no contact with nature except through the eye. But the seat of these perceptions is not the heavens or the æther, but the human organism; and even if the human organism were composed of these or of other such perceptions, the conditions for the existence of these elements and their relation to the heavens, the æther, and one another, would constitute a material world. A psychological nature might thus be ascribed to matter, in its unapproachable internal essence; but that hypothesis, or rather myth, would materialise a late human idea, removed by the whole diameter of evolution and mundane time from the primeval matter which was its object; an object which cannot be found in the landscape of intuition, but must be posited in action, from the outside, in its dynamic and truly material capacity. Criticism, I think, would induce us to stop with this functional definition of matter, which represents our actual approach to it. We should then attach the landscape of intuition to matter only at the summit of evolution, when the psyche becomes a poet, and learns to transcribe her material passions and experiences into terms of essence.

All these partialities in the conception of matter are honest and inevitable. Each view, in stretching its special language as far as possible, may serve to disclose some side of the true order of nature. But this order is that of actual generation and existential flux, something that happens and is not conceived; so that no sensuous or graphic or mathematical transcript of it should be so pressed as to be substituted for it. Nor is it reasonable for those familiar with one side of nature to deride those who, seeing some different side, unsuspectingly identify it with the substance before them. They are wrong; but the critic would be wrong also if he did not tolerate their error, and even prize it for its measure of subjective truth.

The realm of matter, then, from the point of view of our discovery of it, is the field of action: it is essentially dynamic and not pictorial. Moreover, our action is interpolated in a world already in existence. Our existence and purposes are things of yesterday; they were evidently drawn from that very world on which they react. From the point of view of origins, therefore, the realm of matter is the matrix and the source of everything: it is nature, the sphere of genesis, the universal mother. The truth cannot dictate to us the esteem in which we shall hold it: that is not a question of fact but of preference. Yet natural philosophy may disclose the source of our preferences and their implications, so that it may lead us to reconsider them, or to express them differently. So if, with this conception of the realm of matter before us, we turn back to the moral prejudices against matter, we shall be amazed at their levity. A spiritual mind might well look over the head of nature to a First Cause, and beyond the vicissitudes of life to a supreme good: therein there would be a genuine aversion from the realm of matter, and absorption in essences which, at best, existence can illustrate or suggest for a moment to the mind, as it does beauty or the laws of number. But, though not prized for itself, the realm of matter would remain standing; otherwise those divine essences would never have been illustrated or suggested at all. If in clinging to the immaterial we denied the material, it would not be merely ashes or dust that we should be despising, but all natural existence in its abysmal past and in its indefinite fertility; and it would be, not some philosopher's sorry notion of matter that we should be denying, but the reality of our animal being, the fact that we are creatures of time, rooted in a moving universe in which our days are numbered. And rather than blaspheme in this way against our own nature and origin, we might well say with the Irish poet:[1]

> Who is that goddess to whom men should pray,
> But her from whom their hearts have turned away,
> Out of whose virgin being they were born,
> Whose mother-nature they have named with scorn,
> Calling her holy substance common clay. . . .
>
> Ah, when I think this earth on which I tread
> Hath borne these blossoms of the lovely dead,
> And makes the living heart I love to beat,
> I look with sudden awe beneath my feet—

---

[1] " A. E." (George Russell) in " The Virgin Mother ".

and here the poet adds the questionable line:

As you with erring reverence overhead.

If I look overhead, I see the cosmic spaces, the sun or the stars: all this is as much a part of nature, and a source of life, as the nether earth. Or if by " overhead " we understand the spiritual sphere, why should it not be looked upon with as much respect as that realm of matter which, for a free spirit, can be only a means and an instrument? But I think I understand what the poet means, and the justness of his sentiment. *Reverence* is something due to antiquity, to power, to the roots and the moral supports of existence; it is therefore due really to the realm of matter only, and there is a profound error and self-deception in attributing those genetic functions, or directing that piety, to ideal objects. Towards these the appropriate feeling is not reverence so much as love, enthusiasm, contemplative rapture, mystic union: feelings which it would be as silly to address to matter as to address a dutiful reverence to essences or to attribute power to them. In reality, the realm of matter contains more than half of that which from the dawn of life has been the object of human religion: it contains " the gods ", or the veritable influences represented by their names and conciliated by the worship of them. Hell and heaven, for any honest and serious religion, are parts of nature; if ever they cease to be so regarded, they are immediately replaced, as among liberal Protestants, by the goods and evils of this world. The residue of human religion is something private, generous, and not obligatory: it rises from the earth in incense and music, never to return; it forms a spiritual life, akin to poetic love, to happiness, to philosophy.   In contrast with it, the tremendous sanctions and fixed duties of established religion, being instinct with prudence and great hopes, belong to the sober economy of life; and they all regard, if people's eyes were only unsealed, this despised realm of matter.

CONTENTS

xv

CHAPTER I

THE SCOPE OF NATURAL PHILOSOPHY

THE measure of confidence with which I have spoken of essence forsakes me when I approach existence. Logic, grammar, and poetry are free; no alien fact, no vociferation, can prevent intuition from beholding what it actually beholds. The public censor has indeed some rights over Contrast between ideal and natural science. the persons in whom intuition arises, and may condemn their habit of mind if he thinks that it comports idleness or the disruption of happy national conventions; but, in this instance, fortune having relegated me, like the gods of Epicurus, to the interstices of the worlds, I may escape that censure or disregard it. Who knows? Perhaps some kindred spirit may tell me that I have chosen the better part. In any case, I deny nothing and prejudge nothing concerning the intuitions of others; if I cultivate my own with a certain ardour, it is only as any man cultivates his language and tastes, if his mind is at all liberal; and I am confident no god or man will be justly angry with me for browsing so innocently in my own pasture. But when the active impulse of curiosity and dogmatism asserts itself in its turn, as it must in the most contemplative mind, and I ask myself what dark objects or forces have created or are threatening my contemplation, then indeed I am at a loss: and as in positing such natural agencies at all I assume that they are objects obligatory to every

B

other mind with which I can communicate, I bind myself to make my opinions conformable with their reports, and my reports agreeable to their experience. Of course the belief that I can communicate with other minds, and that the reports reaching me signify an experience of theirs over and above my own, is a part of this extraordinary compulsory assumption which I make in living; the assumption that I am surrounded by a natural world, peopled by creatures in whom intuition is as rife as in myself: and as all my concern in perception and action turns on what those external things may do, so half my interest in my own thoughts turns on what other people may be thinking.

    It is not the task of natural philosophy to justify this assumption, which indeed can never be justified. Its task, after making that assumption, is to carry it out consistently and honestly, so as to arrive, if possible, at a conception of nature by which the faith involved in action may be enlightened and guided. Such a description of nature, if it were ever completed in outline, would come round full circle, and in its account of animals it would report how they came to have intuitions (among them this natural philosophy) and to use them in the description of the world which actually surrounded them. The whole field of action and of facts would then be embraced in a single view, summary and symbolic, but comprehensive.

    The dream of the natural philosopher would be to describe the world from its beginning (if it had a beginning), tracing all its transformations; and he would like to do this analytically, not pictorially—that is, not in the sensuous language of some local observer composing a private perspective, but in terms of the ultimate elements (if there are ultimate elements) concerned in the actual evolution of things. Out of those elements he would conceive each observer

Assumption of an existing world.

Inevitable attempt to describe it.

and his perspective arising, and of course varying from moment to moment. Even if the natural philosopher were an idealist, and admitted only observing spirits and their perspectives, he would endeavour to trace the evolution of these intuitions, which would be his atoms, in their universal order and march, by no means contenting himself with one intuition and one perspective; for, if he did so, his idealism (like that of some philosophies of history) would not be a system of physics or of logic, but a literary entertainment, the lyrical echo of many verbal reports in a romantic imagination. This echo might be interesting in itself: but it would remain only an incident in that natural world which indeed it presupposed, but which it deliberately ignored. So that when the idealist became a man again in the world of action, and began to live (as he must) by animal faith, his philosophy would entirely forsake him; yet it is in the service of this animal faith that philosophy exists, when it is science and wisdom. Indeed, a theoretical refusal to trust natural philosophy cannot absolve the most sceptical of us from framing one, and from living by it. I *must* conceive a surrounding world, even if in reflection I say to myself at every step: Illusion, Illusion. It then becomes almost as interesting to know what sort of illusions must accompany me through life, as it would be to imagine what sort of world I really live in. Indeed, if all spurious substitutes for natural philosophy were discarded (spurious because irrelevant to the animal faith which alone posits existence) those two positions might coincide, since the picture of the natural world framed by common sense and science, while framed with the greatest care, would be admittedly only a picture; and belief in the existence of that world, though assumed without wobbling, would be admittedly but an article of inevitable faith.

Non-scientific beliefs about existence, whether inspired by religious feeling, reasoning, or fancy, are

alternatives to the current natural philosophy, or extensions of it. Nobody would believe in his ideas if
Positive religions involve cosmologies. he had not an initial propensity to believe in things, as if his ideas described them. Dogmatic religions are assertions about the nature of the universe; what is called supernatural is only ultra-mundane, an extension of this world on its own plane, and a recognition of forces ruling over it not reckoned with in vulgar commerce. The assertions made by such religious faith, if not superstitious errors, are ultimate truths of natural philosophy, which intuition or revelation has supplied in advance of experiment: but if the assertions are true at all, experiment might one day confirm them. Thus Christian orthodoxy maintains that men will carry their memories and their bodies with them into hell or heaven. Theology is the natural philosophy of that larger world which religion posits as truly existing: it therefore has precise implications in politics and science. The absence of such implications and commitments, far from showing that religion has become spiritual, proves it a sham; it is no longer a manly hypothesis, honestly made about the world confronted in action. No doubt there is an inner fountain of religious feeling which a person accepting his theology on hearsay might wholly lack; but it was religious instinct of some kind that originally prompted those hypotheses about the hidden nature of things, and if this instinct is lacking those hypotheses will soon be discarded. On the other hand, religious feeling may not always require ultra-mundane extensions of the natural world; it may find a sufficient object and sanction in the course of earthly history and domestic life, as was the case, at bottom, with Jewish and Protestant righteousness: the politics and science dictated by religious faith will then coincide with those recommended by worldly wisdom.

Religious feeling may take still other forms; for instance, it may smile mystically at action and belief altogether, retreating into the invisible sanctuary of the spirit, or floating incredulously amid mere music and dreams. But mysticism, whether austere or voluptuous, since it regards the absolute, ceases to regard existence which, by definition, is relative, since it consists in having external relations. Positive and virile minds may find indulgence in such mysticism irreligious, because their earnestness is directed upon alleged facts, in this world or in another: facts essentially relevant to action and policy, and open to natural philosophy.

Much restraint, and some disillusion, may enable a man to entertain ideas without believing them to describe any matter of fact: such ideas will be avowedly mere terms of grammar, logic, or fancy, to be discarded, or at least discounted, on broaching a serious natural philosophy.

Idolatrous character of metaphysics.

They may still be indispensable as a medium, as some language is indispensable to science; but they will be optional and interchangeable, as the scientific part of a book of science (which is never the whole of it) is perfectly translatable from one language into another. This is not to say that the medium of intuition, even in natural philosophy, is indifferent in itself; nothing is dearer to a man or a nation than congenial modes of expression; I would rather be silent than use some people's language; I would rather die than think as some people think. But it is the quality of life that is concerned here, not the truth of ideas. To attempt to impose such modes of intuition or expression, as if they were obligatory tenets, is metaphysics: a projection of the constraints or the creations of thought into the realm of matter. The authority of intuition would be entire if it kept to the definition of essences, and of their essential relations; but when zeal intervenes, and we profess to find our favourite dialectic in things, we are betrayed into disrespect for nature, and are inflating our egotism into cosmic proportions. At best the metaphysician has given a useful hint to the naturalist: he has supplied categories which may be convenient or even indispensable for expressing the ways of nature in human discourse. The palmary instance of this is mathematics, which, long after having ceased to be empirical and become dialectical, still continues to serve for construction and even for prophecy in the material sphere: yet the symbols employed grow more abstruse and tenuous as they grow more exact, so that people are little tempted to substitute the notation for the thing denoted; and they thus escape metaphysics.

When the experience interpreted is spiritual or passionate, the categories used are, as in religion and poetry, clearly mythological: yet they are not without a real, though indirect, object in the realm of matter. This object is the psyche, with all those profound currents in her life which create the passions, and create the spirit which expresses the passions, yet which in expressing them is so entangled that it often comes to regard them as its enemies. Those psychic currents, being dynamic, are material; but they are hidden from the eye of spirit, which alone is spiritual, by layer upon layer of vague sensation, rhetoric, and imagery.

Belief, in its very soul, is belief about nature; it is animal faith. To entangle belief in anything non-natural, or avowedly tangential to action, would be to cheat at the game. Honest speculative belief is always speculative physics. But its terms are inevitably the essences present to intuition; and the very faith which, in the presence of these essences, posits existing things, drags something of the given apparition into the presumed

Nature is the nexus of all substances and forces.

substance of the thing revealed: the theophany humanises the god. In correcting this illusion, and in discarding one mythical or metaphysical image after another, science must still retain some symbol for the overpowering reality of the world. This reality is not that symbol itself, nor a collection of such symbols: if we cling to these we shall never quit the realm of essence. Nor am I sure that the most learned symbols are the least deceptive; if any human ideas must be idolized, I should almost prefer those of the senses and of the poets. Yet it would be ignominious for a philosopher voluntarily to succumb to illusion at all, when the artificiality and relativity of all human views, especially of learned and beautiful systems, is so patent to reflection. Yet views we must have, none the worse, surely, if they are beautiful and learned; so that the natural philosopher is driven to a deeper question, to which I mean to devote this book: How much, when cleared as far as possible of idolatry, can sense or science reveal concerning the dark engine of nature? In what measure do they truly enlighten animal faith?

In broaching this question I am not concerned with repeating, correcting, or forecasting the description which men of science may give of the world. How far is I accept gladly any picture of nature honestly science drawn by them, as I accept gladly any picture knowledge? drawn by my own senses. Different circumstances or different faculties would certainly have produced different pictures. From Genesis to Thales, to Ptolemy, to Copernicus, to Newton, and to Einstein the landscape has pleasantly varied; and it may yet open other vistas. These variations and prospects show the plasticity of human thought, for it is not the facts that have much varied, nor the material station of man, nor his senses and destiny. The incubus of existence remains exactly the same. Is it merely imagination that has become more laboured but no less fantastic? Or has the path of destiny been really cleared and the forces that control destiny been better understood? Within what limits does any description of nature, picturesque or scientific, retain its relevance to animal faith and its validity as knowledge of fact, and at what point does it become pure speculation and metaphor? That is the only question which I shall endeavour to answer.

My survey of the realm of matter will accordingly be merely transcendental, and made from the point of view of a sceptic and a moralist criticising the claims of experience and science to be true knowledge.

By transcendental reflection I understand reversion, in the presence of any object or affirmation, to the immediate experience which discloses that object or prompts that affirmation. Transcendental reflection is a challenge to all dogmatism, a demand for radical evidence. It therefore tends to disallow substance and, when it is thorough, even to disallow existence. Nothing is ultimately left except the passing appearance or the appearance of something passing. How, then, if transcendental reflection disallows substance, can it lead me to distinguish the properties of substance?

The transcendental method applied to animal faith.

In *Scepticism and Animal Faith* I have considered the transcendental motives which oblige me to believe in substance. The belief must always remain an assumption, but one without which an active and intelligent creature cannot honestly act or think. Transcendentalism has two phases or movements—the sceptical one retreating to the immediate, and the assertive one by which objects of belief are defined and marshalled, of such a character and in such an order as intelligent action demands. The enterprise of life is precarious, and to the sceptic it must seem an adventure in the dark, without origins or environment or results. Yet this flying life, by its forward energy, breeds from within certain postulates of sanity, certain conceptions

of the conditions which might surround it and lend it
a meaning, so that its own continuance and fortunes
may be conceived systematically and affirmed with
confidence. Thus the faith that posits and describes
a world is just as transcendental as the criticism which
reduces that world to an appearance or a fiction. If so
many transcendental philosophers stop at the negative
pole, this arrest is not a sign of profundity in them,
but of weakness. It is by boldly believing what transcendental necessity prompts any hunting animal to
believe, that I separate myself from that arrested
idealism, and proceed to inquire what existences, what
substances, and what motions are involved in the chase.

In the chase, for those who follow it, the intensity
of experience is not like the intensity (limitless if you
will) of contemplating pure Being—immutable,
equable, and complete. The hunter and the *Action
posits a*
hunted believe in something ambushed and *field existing sub-*
imminent: present images are little to them *stantially*
but signs for coming events. Things are *for science
to describe.*
getting thick, agents are coming together,
or disappearing: they are killing and dying. The
assurance of this sort of being is assurance of existence,
and the belief in this sort of agent is belief in substance.
If this belief and assurance are not illusions (which
the acting animal cannot admit them to be), several
properties must belong to substances and to the world
they compose. These properties I may distinguish in
reflection and call by philosophical names, somewhat
as follows.

CHAPTER II

INDISPENSABLE PROPERTIES OF SUBSTANCE

1. Since substance is posited, and not given in intuition, as essences may be given, *substance is external to the thought which posits it.*

2. Since it is posited in action, or in readiness for action, the substance posited is external not merely to the positing thought (as a different thought would be) but is external to the physical agent which is the organ of that action, as well as of that thought. In other words, *Substance has parts and constitutes a physical space.* Conversely, the substantial agent in action and thought is external to the surrounding portions of substance with which it can interact. *All the parts of substance are external to one another.*

A world in which action is to occur must be external, spatial, and temporal, possessing variety and unity.

3. Since substance is engaged in action, and action involves change, *substance is in flux and constitutes a physical time.* Changes are perpetually occurring in the relations of its parts, if not also in their intrinsic characters.

4. Since the agents in action and reaction are distinct in position and variable in character, and since they induce changes in one another, *substance is unequally distributed.* It diversifies the field of action, or physical time and space.

5. Since there is no occasion for positing any

substance save as an agent in the field of action, all recognisable substance must lie in the same field in which the organism of the observer occupies a relative centre. Therefore, wherever it works and solicits recognition, *substance composes a relative cosmos*.

A mutual externality, or *Auseinandersein*—an alternation of centres such as moment and moment, thing and thing, place and place, person and person —is characteristic of existence. Each centre is equally actual and equally central, yet each is dependent on its neighbours for its position and on its predecessors for its genesis. The existential interval from one centre to another is bridged naturally by generation or motion— by a transition actually taking place from one moment, place, or character to another, in such a manner that the former moment, place, or character is abandoned and lost. The same interval may still be bridged cognitively by faith or intent, cognition being a substitute for a transition which cannot be executed materially, because the remote term of it is past or not next in the order of genesis or transformation. But this interval can never be bridged by synthesis in intuition. Synthesis in intuition destroys the existential status of the terms which it unites, since it excludes any alternation or derivation between them. It unites at best the essences of some natural things into an ideal picture. On the other hand the conjunction of existences in nature must always remain successive, external, and unsynthesised. Nature shows no absolute limits and no privileged partitions; whereas the richest intuition, the most divine omniscience, is imprisoned in the essence which it beholds. It cannot break through into existence unless it loses itself and submits to transition; and the foretaste or aftertaste of such transition, present in feeling, must posit something eventual, something absent from intuition, if

The first property, externality to thought belongs to all existence.

even the sense or idea of existence is to arise at all. Then the mind engaged in action may begin to live by faith in the outlying conditions of life, and by an instinctive tension towards obscure events.

It might seem that memory eludes this necessity, and actually encloses some parts of the past in the

Memory, when cognitive, a relation between separate natural facts.

present, and brings the movement of events bodily within the circle of intuition. But this is an illusion founded on the fact that memory contains both imagery and know-ledge: the imagery is all present, but that of which it gives knowledge, when memory is true, is past and gone. Even if, by a rare favour, the original aspect of the past experience should be reproduced exactly, it will not be the past event, nor even the present one, that will be given in intuition, but the dateless essence common to both.

The cognitive value of this apparition will hang on the ulterior fact that such an apparition, or the event which it reports, occurred before, at a point of time which was its own centre, and not a marginal feature in the present perspective. Memory, then, in so far as it is, or even claims to be, knowledge, is faith in the absent, and bridges external relations by intent only, not by synthesis in intuition.

A mutual externality is also requisite among the instances of spirit, that is, among thoughts that are to

Existing thoughts are separate events lodged each in its place in nature.

be regarded as existences and events. This at first sight might seem contrary to the apparent self-existence and self-evidence of conscious being, and to the transcendental status of spirit, which, because it is a logical counterpart to any datum, might be alleged to be an omnipresent fact, existing absolutely. But this, although it may pass for criticism, is the sophistry of reflection, which can readily take its verbal terms for existences or substances, and ignore the natural springs of feeling and of reflection itself. An instance of spirit, a pure feeling or intuition, if it had no date or place in nature, would not be an event or existence at all, but only another name, and a mythical name, for the essence conceived to be present there. The life of thought, in its conscious intensity, lies in the syntheses which it is perpetually making among its changing materials. These acts of synthesis, these glances and insights, are historical facts; they arise and are distinguishable on the level of experience from their material conditions; but they are not substances. Their substance is their organ in its movement and in its changing tensions: it is the psyche. The case is like that of a collision between two vehicles, or check-mate in a game of chess. The collision is a new fact, on the plane of human affairs, as is the checkmate which ends the game; so, too, are the chagrin or the severe pain which these events may occasion. But the pain or the chagrin could no more arise, or come into existence, without the living persons who endure them—persons moving in the realm of matter—than the checkmate could occur without the match, or the collision without the vehicles. If a feeling or thought is to be actual, and not a metaphorical name for some eternal essence, it must therefore arise out of material events, and in the midst of them: it must stand in external relations.

Thus the first indispensable condition for the being of substance is indispensable also to any form of existence, mental or historical as well as physical. Existence, like substance, is essentially diffuse and many-centred. One fact can be reached cognitively from another fact only by faith, and materially only by transition; and the cognitive or the initial fact itself can exist only by virtue of its position or action in a natural system extending beyond it.

It follows that substance is in flux, virtual, if not actual. External relations are such as are due to the

Existence being con- tingent is essentially unstable.

position, not to the inherent character, of the terms. They are, therefore, always variable, and existence, although it may endure by accident for any length of time, is inherently mortal and transitory, being adventitious to the essences which figure in it. When Hamlet says, *To be or not to be*, he is pondering the alternative between existence and non-existence, and feeling the contingency of both. The question is not whether he shall be or not be Hamlet: death might cause him to forget his essence, but could not abolish it or transform it into another essence. In the realm of essence all these essences are eternally present and no alternative arises: which is perhaps the ultimate truth conveyed by the doctrine of eternal salvation or punishment. But the accidents of death, or dreams, or oblivion continually confront this life, and existence is an optional form of being. Shall this beloved or detested essence presently lose it? And on what other essence shall it fall next? To this pressing question the realm of essence supplies no answer, and the contemplative mind is hopelessly puzzled by it. *Solvitur ambulando*: the event, the pro-pulsive currents of substance merging and rushing into new forms, will precipitate a solution without ever considering alternatives; and it is perhaps because they never stop to think before they act, that they are able to act at all.

Something not essence, then, actualises and limits the manifestation of every essence that figures

The sub- stance which de- termines events is itself in motion.

in nature or appears before the mind. To this dark principle of existence we give the name of substance; so that substance, by defini-tion, is the soil, the medium, and the creative force which secretly determines any option like that of Hamlet. Every such option is momentary and local; for although substance is external to essence and to thought, and its parts are external to one another, yet substance is internal to the things which it forms by occupying those contrasted places and assuming these various qualities. It is *their* substance, the principle of their existence, the ground of all the spontaneous changes which they undergo. It is indefinitely, perhaps infinitely, deep and inhuman; but whatever else its intrinsic essence may be, it is certainly complex, local, and temporal. Its secret flux involves at least as many contrasts and variations as the course of nature shows on the surface. Otherwise the ultimate core of existence would not exist, and the causes of variation would not vary. But how shall that which puts on this specious essence here and not there, be in the same inner condition in both places? Or how shall that which explodes now, have been equally active before? Substance, if it is to fulfil the function in virtue of which it is recognised and posited, must accordingly be for ever changing its own inner condition. It must be in flux.

Undoubtedly the word substance suggests permanence rather than change, because the substances best known to man (like the milk and the wet sand of the young architect) evidently pass from place to place and from form to form while retaining their continuity and quantity. Such permanence is not contrary to flux, but a condition of flux. The degree of permanence which substance may have in any particular *Permanence need not be attributed to substance otherwise than as implied in flux.* process, and the name which should be given to this permanent factor, are questions for scientific discussion. They may not, and need not, receive any ultimate answer. But that *some* permanence, not the casual persistence of this or that image, is interwoven with the flux of things, follows from the reality of this flux itself. If change were total at any point, there transformation and existence would come to an end. The next, completely new, fact would not be next; it would be the centre, or the beginning, of a separate world. In other words, events, if they are to be successive or contiguous, must be pervaded by a common medium, in which they may assume relations external to their respective essences; for the internal or logical relations between these essences will never establish any succession or continuity among them, nor transport them at all into the sphere of existence. The critics of empiricism who have insisted that a series of sensations is not the sensation of a series, might well have added that the sensation of a series is no more than an isolated term on its own account, unless there is a background common to those terms and to this synthetic idea—a background in relation to which they may respectively take such places as shall render them contiguous or successive, although there is nothing within any of them to indicate such a position. This background, for human perception, is the field of vision symbolising the field of action; in this specious field the position of objects is distinguished before the objects are clearly specified or posited; but this unity of perspective, relative to the momentary station and thought of the observer, cannot embrace the existential flux itself, in which the events reported and the observer, with his thought, are incidental features. For the continuity and successiveness of this existing series, synthesis in apprehension is useless: it merely creates one more item—a living thought—to be ranged among its neighbours in the flux of existence. That which is requisite is the *natural derivation* of one phase in this flux from another, or a *natural tension* between them, determining their respective characters and positions. Such derivation and such tension, essential to action, involve a substance within or between events. There may be very much more in substance than that; but this is enough to disclose the existence of a substance, and to begin the human description of it by its functions.

Permanence, therefore, need not be set down separately among the radical properties attributed to substance: it is sufficiently expressed in the possibility of change, of continuity, of succession, and of the inclusion of actual events in a natural series, which shall not be a mere perspective in imagination.

Action and animal faith look in some specific direction; the butt of action, which is what I call substance, must be particular, local, and circumscribed. It must be capable of varying its position or its condition; for otherwise I could neither affect it by my action, nor await and observe *Action presupposes a diversified field.* its operation. In battle, in the chase, or in labour, attention is turned to a particular quarter, to something substantial there: it would defeat all action and art if all quarters were alike, and if I couldn't face a fact without turning my back on exactly the same fact in the rear; and the price of bread would be indifferent, if one substance being everywhere present I could find the same substance in the air. Action evidently would be objectless in an infinite vacuum or a homogeneous plenum; and even the notion or possibility of action would vanish if I, the agent, had not distinguishable parts, so that at least I might swim forward rather than backward in that dense vacuity.

A field of action must, then, be diversified substantially, not pictorially only; that which is at work in it here must not be equally at work in it there; the opportunities which it opens to me now must not be the same which it opened and will open always. Any conception of substance which represents it as undivided and homogeneous is accordingly not a conception of nature or of existence: and if *The substance of things is physical: metaphysical substance is only a grammatical term.* such an object is ever called substance, it must be in

C

a metaphysical sense which I do not attach to the word.
One test of such evasions into the realm of essence is
ability, or ambition, to give a precise definition of what
substance is. *Materia prima* may be defined—Plotinus
has an admirable exposition of it, like the Athanasian
creed—because it is avowedly something incapable of
existence, and at best one of those ideal terms which
serve to translate nature into the language of thought.
Materia prima is a grammatical essence, comparable
to the transcendental ego, the " I think ", which according to Kant must accompany all experience. The
discrimination of such essences distinguishes one logic
from another, and leaves everything in nature, except
human language, just as it was. The existing substance
of things, on the contrary, is that which renders them
dynamic; it is wherever dynamic things are, not where
they are not; it determines their aspects and powers;
and we may learn, since it exists in us also, to play with
it and to let it play on us, in specific ways. But it
would be frivolous to attempt to define it, as if a set
of words, or of blinking ideas, could penetrate to the
heart of existence and determine how, from all eternity,
it must have been put together. What we may discover
of it is not its essence but its place, its motion, its
aspects, its effects. Were it an essence given in intuition, a visionary presence to sense or to language, it
would forfeit those very functions which compel us to
posit it, and which attest its formidable reality. Chief
of these functions is a perpetual and determinate revolution in the heavens, and fertility and decay upon earth.
In this flux there is a relative permanence and continuity; but substance is not for that reason less agitated than the familiar face of nature, or nearer to the
impassibility of an eternal essence. Far otherwise.
Investigation rather shows that this substance (which
may be traced experimentally in many of its shifts) is
in a continual silent ferment, by which gross visible

objects are always being undermined and transformed: so much so that science often loses its way amid those subtle currents of the elements, and stops breathless at some too human image.

There are certain celebrated doctrines which, in their forms of expression, are excluded at once from natural philosophy by these considerations. In physics I may not say, for instance, with Parmenides Parmenides that Being is and Not-Being is not, if what must give way to I am seeking to describe is the substance of Democritus. nature. If for dialectical reasons, which are not directly relevant to physics, I wished to regard pure Being as the essence of matter, I should be compelled to distribute this pure Being unequally in a void: a result which would contradict my premise that Not-Being is not, since this void would not only exist but would be the only true theatre of existence, because it would be the only seat of change. The pure Being or matter distributed in it, by hypothesis, is impassible and everywhere identical. Nature and life would therefore be due to the redistribution in the bosom of Not-Being of a pure Being in itself immutable. We should thus be led to the system of Democritus: a possible and even a model system of physics, although, in its expression, too Eleatic, and borrowing from that dialectical school a false air of necessity.

Similarly, at the threshold of natural philosophy, the Vedanta system must yield to the Samkhya: and this the Indians seem to have admitted by The Ve- regarding the two systems as orthodox and danta must compatible. It might be well if in the West give way we could take a hint from this comprehensive- Samkhya ness. The unity and simplicity of pure Being system. is not incompatible with the infinite variety of essences implied in it; and many things are true in the realm of essence which, if taken to describe existence, would be unmeaning or contrary to fact. It would suffice to distinguish the two spheres more carefully, for the legitimacy of systems, verbally most unlike, to become equal: although certainly those which were drawn from insight into essence would be more profound and unshakable than those drawn from observation of nature, since nature might as well have offered quite a different spectacle. On the other hand, it is the order and ground of this spectacle that interests the natural philosopher; and to him that more inward and more sublime intuition of essential Being is a waste of time, or a rhetorical danger.

One more illustration: the language of Spinoza about substance ought to yield, in physics, to that of Aristotle, in spite of the fact that a follower of Descartes could not help being more enlightened in mechanical matters than a follower of Socrates. Nevertheless it was

And Spinoza must give way to Aristotle.

Aristotle who gave the name of substance to compound natural things actually existing, and Spinoza who bestowed it on an ambiguous metaphysical object, now pure Being, now the universe in its infinity—in either case an ideal unity and an essence incapable of realisation all at once, if at all, in any natural locus. No discrimination of infinite Being into infinitely numerous attributes would ever generate existence, since all would remain eternal; and no enumeration of the possible modes of each attribute would turn them into particular things or into living minds, since each mode would imply all the others, and all would be equally rooted everywhere. In Aristotle, on the contrary, the name of substance is given where the office of substance is performed, and where one fact here asserts itself against another fact there; so that substance is the principle of individuation and exclusion, the condition of existence, succession, and rivalry amongst natural things. Even if these things, as conceived by Aristotle, have too much of an animate unity, and are mysteriously fixed in their genera and species, and redolent of moral suggestions, all this is but the initial dramatic rendering of their human uses, and the poetry of good prose. It does not prevent a more disinterested analysis, a microscopic and telescopic science, from disclosing in time the deeper mechanisms and analogies of nature, and its finer substance: just as the static zoology and the political psychology of Aristotle do not prevent us from peeping into the seething elementary passions beneath those classical masks. Things have not ceased to wear the sensuous and moral forms which interested the Greeks; but we may discover how those shells were generated, and what currents of universal substance have cast them up.

Finally, the practical intellect, in positing substance, imposes on it a certain relevance to the agent, who is to be in dynamic relations with it. The objects which art and sanity compel me to recognise as substantial, must affect me together, even if in very different ways. They must all impinge, directly or indirectly, on my action now; and it is by this test that I distinguish fact from fiction and true memory from fancy. Facts are dynamically connected with that which I now posit as substantial, and objects of fancy are not so connected. The field of animal faith spreads out from a living centre; observation cannot abandon its base, but from this vital station it may extend its perspectives over everything to which it can assign existence. Among these accredited things there may be other centres of observation, actual or eventual; but if the original organ and station, and these other stations and organs accredited by it, were not parts of one and the same substantial world, no means would remain of identifying the objects observed from one centre with those observed from another. I can acknowledge the existence

The field of action must have a dynamic unity.

of other moral centres in the world which I posit, but only if these centres are agencies, earthly or celestial, at work in my field of action, and dynamically connected with my own existence. All credible animation, of ascertainable character, must animate substances found in the same world with myself, and collateral with my own substance.

Perhaps this argument has some analogy to Spinoza's proof of the unity of substance. He tells us that substance is one, because if there were two or more substances they could bear no relation to one another. In other words, there can be but one universe, since anything outside, by being outside, would be related to it and collateral, and so after all would form a part of it. Yet if one universe, or one substance, can exist absolutely, and out of all relation to anything else, why should not any number of them exist, each centred in itself? The necessity of lying in external relations in order to exist, far from proving that only one system of facts is possible, proves that any closed circle of facts, in interplay with one another and with nothing else, will form a complete universe. Each part of this system will exist by virtue of its active position there, and may be discovered by any members of it who are sufficiently intelligent and adventurous; but from no part of that universe will anything beyond that universe be discoverable. Does this fact preclude the being of a different system, a separate universe, possessing the same sort of inward life and reality? I cannot think so. Transcendental necessities are relative to particular centres of experience; they have no jurisdiction beyond. Those other universes, to us, would be undiscoverable; but ours, too, would be undiscoverable to them; and yet we exist here without their leave. Might they not exist without ours?

What logic enables us to assert, therefore, is not

This system is relative and need not cover all reality.

that there is only one universe, but that each universe must be one, by virtue of a domestic economy determining the relative position and character of the events which compose it. Anything beyond this dynamic field is beyond the field of posited existence and possible knowledge. If there are other centres and active substances moving in other spheres, the relation of these disconnected spheres is not a physical relation: no journey and no transformation can bridge it: it lies in the realm of truth. Each of these worlds will exemplify its chosen essence; and the internal and unchangeable relations *If there are many worlds their mutual relations are not physical, but are the eternal relations of their essences in the realm of truth.* between these essences will be the only relations between those worlds. One will not exist before the other, nor will they be simultaneous; nor will either lie in any direction from the other, or at any distance. No force or influence will pass between them of any traceable physical or historical kind. If omniscience should see any harmony, contrast, or mutual fulfilment between their natures, that spiritual bond would be of the sort which links essences together by a logical necessity, and which a contemplative spirit may stop to disentangle and admire if it can and will.

Indeed, we may go further and say even of a single universe taken as a whole that its status is that of a truth rather than of an existence. Each part of it will exist, and if animate may truly feel its internal tension and life, and may truly assert the existence of the other parts also; yet the whole system—perhaps endless in its time and space—never exists at once or in any assignable quarter. Its existence is only posited from within its limits: externally its only status is that of a truth. Its essence was not condemned to be a closet-tragedy; living actors have been found to play it and a shifting stage to exhibit for a moment those convincing scenes. This essence has therefore the eternal dignity of a truth: it is the complete description of an event. Yet this event, taken as a whole, being unapproachable from outside, dateless, and nowhere, is in a sense a supernatural event. Those scenes are undiscoverable, save to those who play them, and that tumult is an ancient secret in the bosom of truth.

Indeed, good sense might suffice to convince anyone that no arguments or definitions can prevent things from being as numerous and as separate as they may chance to be. There is an infinite diversity of essences: what shall dissuade the fatality of existence, which must be groundless, from composing such changeful systems as it likes, on planes of being utterly incommensurable and incommunicable? The most a man can say for himself, or for any other element from which exploration may start, is that whatever is to enter his field of action must belong to the same dynamic system with himself. In experience and art, as in the nebular hypothesis, this dynamic oneness of the world is primitive. It is not put together by conjoining elements found existing separately, but is the locus in which they are found; for if they were not found there, they would be essences only and not facts. In mature human perception the essences given are doubtless distinct and the objects which they suggest are clearly discriminated: here is the dog, there the sun, the past nowhere, and the night coming. But beneath all this definition of images and attitudes of expectancy, there is always a voluminous feeble sensibility in the vegetative soul. Even this sensibility posits existence; the contemplation of pure Being might supervene only after all alarms, gropings, and beliefs had been suspended—something it takes all the discipline of Indian sages to begin to do. The vegetative soul enjoys an easier and more Christian blessedness: it sees not, yet it believes. But believes in what? In

The first object of animal faith is nature as a whole.

whatever it may be that envelopes it; in what we, in our human language, call space, earth, sunlight, and motion; in the throbbing possibility of putting forth something which we call leaves, for which that patient soul has no name and no image. The unknown total environment is what every intellect posits at birth; whatever may be attempted in action or discovered in nature will be a fresh feature in that field. Everything relevant to mortal anxiety lies within that immensity, be it an object of earthly fear or pursuit or of religious hope. Animal faith and material destiny move in a relative cosmos.

CHAPTER III

PRESUMABLE PROPERTIES OF SUBSTANCE

THE properties which, willy-nilly, we assign to substance by trusting it and by presuming to act upon it, are relative and functional properties. Has substance no other properties, positive and native to it, which we may discover by observation or experience?

That substance has many native and positive characters is certain: in its diffusion it lends existence to certain eternal essences, and enables them to figure in a flux of events. At each point, then, substance must exemplify some essence, of which, then and there, it creates an instance; but it does so by setting that essence in a frame of external relations; so that substance is always more and other than the essence which it exemplifies at any point. It is also more than the set of external relations, or the natural medium, into which these exchangeable essences fall; for this framework, apart from the exchange of alternative essences which diversify it and individuate its parts, would itself be a mere essence, like geometrical space or time, eternal and unsubstantial. This is not to say that, besides the essences which it exemplifies at each point, and the manner in which it connects and exchanges them, substance need have any *other* essence of its own. Its residual being, or not-being, is antithetical to essence altogether, and irrational. We may

Besides its necessary functions, substance manifests many positive properties.

enjoy it, we may enact it, but we cannot conceive it; not because our intellect by accident is inadequate, but because existence, which substance makes continuous, is intrinsically a surd, a flux, and a contradiction.

The question for the natural philosopher is therefore reduced to this: which, if any, of the essences revealed in human experience or observation may we assign to substance and regard as belonging to its essence?

This question might be answered easily and rather gloriously in a single word, All! Every character, every relation, every event which occurs anywhere qualifies substance and is a property of it. We should thus come at once upon a perfectly correct, if perfectly useless, definition of substance: the essence of substance would be that of the universe, or so much of the realm of essence as is ever exemplified in existence, when, where, and in the manner in which it is exemplified. This definition, I say, would be correct, because the essences which substance takes on in detail are certainly forms of substance at those points; while those essences which it takes on in its larger sweeps (or, as I shall call them, its tropes) are forms of substance on that scale and in those cycles. In this way a man is a substance, because his human and his personal essence have become forms of substance in him; and the universe is the sum of all substance, the form of which is called the truth. Even those instances of essence which are not forms of substance in this passive manner, are manifestations of substance by way of active expression or epigenesis; though not embodied in substance they are evoked from it and compose the realm of spirit, which is a natural manifestation of substance in man, but not a true description of it. The freest intuition is free only outwards, in that, like music, it need not look towards substance or towards truth; but, like music, the freest

All exemplified essences are in some respect qualities of substance.

intuition is closely bound to substance by its genesis, and rooted there altogether; so that all the essences appearing in contemplation belong to the essence of substance, as all the subtlest developments of music or dialectic belong to the essence of man.

Nevertheless the proposed definition of substance would be useless: it would merely say that all that exists exists, without indicating what is its tenure of existence or the mode of its attachment to substance; and this is the question which arises in action and which gives the category of substance its meaning. Indeed, if from the truth that all phenomena are manifestations of substance, in some direction and at some remove, we passed to the idea that all phenomena are equally substantial, we should have fallen into a positive error; and the word substance itself would have become superfluous; which is the reason why modern philosophers have dropped it. Not that in dropping the word they have abandoned the category: something somewhere must exist in itself and be substantial; but this self-existence would be made to migrate from the heart of things to their surface, or to the total picture which they make in the mind's eye, or to this mind's eye itself, assumed though perhaps not mentioned. Any of these dislocations of substance would render it irrelevant to action. Action cannot accept phenomena simply as phenomena, but must trace the substantial thread on which they are strung together; for it is quite false that any phenomenon taken in itself is substantial; it is a mere essence, save for its backing in nature, which, although it always exists, is often very recondite, and definable by essences very different from that which it wears on the surface.

The dog in the fable, who dropped the substance for the shadow, might have found substance even in that shadow, namely, water and light reflected from the

But none is a substance in itself.

water; and if he had been a natural philosopher, he might have traced that ray back to the very bone which he had held in his mouth, and had let slip for   The dog the sake of its deceptive image. This com-   and the plication in the manifestations of substance   bone. misled his action, because he was not interested in manifestations at all, but only in a substance which he might assimilate blindly and turn into the hidden substance of himself: and *this* substance was not to be found where he sought it. There is a natural hierarchy in the manifestations of substance; and while no appearance is a mere appearance, but all are in some way appearances of substance, yet some of the essences exhibited to human intuition fit the dynamic movement of nature tightly and consecutively, and can be true guides to action, whereas others are poised delicately there, like a mood or a dream, not long to be traced or trusted; for the flux of substance has other forms beneath to which it proves more faithful. While we halt and disport ourselves at the human level, substance slips on in its merely material career, and that poem is ended. The study of substance is the pursuit of these deepest and most pervasive of its properties, and of the manner in which the rarer properties and the supervening unities are generated in that context. It is the study of physics.

In dreams substance mocks the pursuer; he wastes the emotions of action in a direction in which substance is absent, and action therefore impossible;   Pharaoh's but in another direction, namely, in himself,   dream. substance is always at hand, and he may ironically trace his dream back to it on waking. Pharaoh's dream was all about substance, yet much interpretation was needed before his fat and lean kine could disclose their relevance to the world of action. They had such relevance initially in his royal preoccupation with animals and with the fat of the land; but this backward reference of ideas to their seat and their origin is seldom conveyed by the deliverance of the ideas themselves; when it is, they become reflection or memory. In the forward impulse of perception or policy, ideas have, or are taken to have, a forward reference to substance as well: appetition turns them into prophecies. Fortunately Pharaoh had at his elbow a prophetic materialist, to whom ideas were signs, and who readily conceived what genuine substances might be signified by them; and the event having justified his prudent guess, the statesman needed to go no further in his interpretation of ideas: the people's stomach and the king's treasury were ultimate substances for him. Had Joseph been a more curious philosopher, even a treasury or a stomach might have seemed to him but covering ideas, standing for undeciphered operations of nature; and he might have begun to speculate about earth and water, the sun and the miracle of seeds; but even if his science had advanced as far as the science of to-day, it would not have reached anything but some more abstract term, or more refined covering idea. He had found substance, as substance may be found, in the thick of action, in those harvests and granaries; there he had touched the hand of the Lord.

There is another fable which renders the matter more subtly, and dwells more on its ideal side. Nar-

Narcissus.   cissus was not deceived like the dog; he knew that the fair image was but a reflection of himself; but in his love of form he was seized with a sort of desperate enthusiasm, and coveted that celestial object with an earthly passion; so that his fate was worse than the dog's, and in plunging after the shadow he lost not only that fancied substance, but his true substance and life as well. Not that self-love need always be suicidal. Had Narcissus been content to enjoy his own substance blindly, in its coursing life through his members, he might have possessed himself mightily and long, being all action, all ignorance, all irresponsibility; he might have reverted from the Narcissus of fable to the Narcissus of Freud. But the poets have made him a symbol for a higher fate, for the great deviation of attention from substance to essence. This deviation, as we see in him, has two stages, one confused and mad, at which he stopped, and another sublime and musical, to which he might have proceeded. For Narcissus is the forerunner of Apollo, or Apollo in embryo; he explains the mystery of Apollo having been born so free and so deeply inspired; for high things must have deep and hidden foundations. The foundation of intuition, and of all the free arts, lies in the substance of the self, with its long vegetable and animal evolution; until one day, in the person of Narcissus, attention is arrested on the form which the self lends to all nature, or wears in its own eyes. If at first this intuition is not pure, and Narcissus wildly pursues essence as if it were substance, he becomes Dionysus, inspired but drunk: if on the contrary his intuition liberates the form of substance from its flux, and sees it in its wholeness and in its unsubstantiality, then Narcissus becomes Apollo, inspired but sane.

These parables have a common moral. Ideas, or the forms which things wear in human experience, are unsubstantial in themselves, cheating every action or hope that may be directed upon them in their literal immediate being, or given essence; but they may all be traced, either by interpretation outwards or by reversion inwards to their origin in the self, until they lead us to substance; that is, to something *However unprecedented their form, all things are traceable by their substance.* that can be the butt of action, and in which the effects of action may be fertile and prolonged. Experience and the arts of life thus seem to justify the presumption that all things are natural, even the most ideal, and that nothing, even in a dream, appears by chance, but that all is symptomatic, significant, and grounded in substance.

And as all things unsubstantial may be traced to substance, so all the movements of substance may be

Which on its own plane is a continuous process. traced to one another. It is sheer ignorance to stare at anything as if it were inexplicable and self-created, a mere intruder in the world. The universe itself no doubt is groundless and a perpetual miracle; but it is a tame wonder, and terribly self-imitative; and everything in it bears its hallmark and stamp of origin, if we only are clever enough to turn it inside out, and inspect its fabric. The habits of nature are marvellous, but they are habits; and the flux of substance fills quite innocently and automatically the intervals which its own lapse may create. This assumption is not justifiable by induction, because no experience covers any great part of nature, nor that part thoroughly; but it is nevertheless the anchor of rational life. All prudence, all art, all calculation rely upon it, and prosper—in so far as they prosper—by that confidence.

The simplest sort of continuity is persistence, or sustained identity: and this is often found or assumed

Some things are traceable because roughly persistent. in the field of action. Leaving my hat and umbrella in the cloak room, I expect, on my departure, to find the same objects. I conceive them to have endured unchanged in the interval. And when I take fresh possession of them, and carry them into quite another place, I conceive that, save for a little wear and tear, they still remain identical. And I assume a similar battered identity in my own person. If things lapsed in nature as they lapse in immediate experience, objects that disappeared at any point would be annihilated, and some new thing, perhaps like them but not the same, would presently be created somewhere else. This magical world may be acceptable to a laughing child, or a desperate sceptic, but it will never do for a sportsman. If the scent is lost for a moment, he must assume that the fox is still in existence, or he could not pursue the chase. To wait and wonder whether another fox might not be created anywhere else at any other time would not be hunting; nor would it be labour, nor art, nor science; it would be treating objects not as substances but as apparitions. That which appears, if it is posited as a thing to be chased, must exist continuously even when it does not appear. The object at each instant must occupy some particular position in the field of action, a place determinable by exploration; and belief and action may be directed upon it when invisible with entire confidence that its path is traceable and calculable.

That substances persist through motion is a veritable postulate of practical reason: not a mock postulate known to be false (as Kant's postulates were apparently meant to be) but one believed to be true, and constantly revived by events. If it were not true, action, and even the thought of action, would be farcical, and would in fact never have arisen. Yet this postulate, as action implies and verifies it, does not extend further than action itself. The huntsman need not assume that his fox will live for ever. Possibly its haunting image, surviving the chase, may of old have suggested to him his totems and animal gods; but in the chase itself only a brief persistence, limited to this particular fox, is posited or proved. Soon this substance is expected to disappear; true, it may feed the hunter or his dogs; yet no theory of a total and absolute indestructibility of substance, through all its transformations, need be broached in practice. The persistence which the human mind tends to attribute to things, especially when they are loved or feared, is less that of their substance than of

Persistence in substance need not be everlasting or universal.

D

their ghosts. It is a confused intermixture of essences with facts, of casual circumstances with profound reverberations in memory. Experience, even in those of us who think ourselves enlightened, is full of increments and losses which seem to us absolute, as if they were souls, strengths, or illuminations coming from other spheres. The field of action remains to that extent an animated chaos in which at best certain magic rhymes may be detected, which superstition raises into laws. Were it not for sane instinct, custom, and the steadying machinery of the arts, we should all be little better than poets. It is but a thin thread of calculable continuity that runs through immediate experience: the postulate of permanence is applicable and reasonable only in the field of action posited outside, and only in so far as exact arts and sciences may be able to dominate it.

Might not substance, then, be as intermittent and spasmodic as experience itself? Might it not be a fire whose very nature was to lapse: not merely to lapse inwardly and devour its own flames, but occasionally to lapse from existence altogether, like the setting sun of Heraclitus? A different sun, he observed, was created in the morning; and perhaps not all the intervals or pauses between existences would be so regular, nor the existences so much alike. Some sun might be the last; it would not follow that it had not existed. So all existence might be occasional, and destined some day to fail altogether. A playful philosopher, now that science has again become playful, might conceive that all things are totally destroyed at each instant, and fresh things created—I was going to say "in their place", but I should rather say in fresh places, since times and spaces in such a system would also have no unity and no continuity. Yet these momentary worlds would still be substantial, in the transcendental sense; they would not be merely

It might exist discretely at separate moments.

phenomenal, if they were independent, while they lasted, of the notice taken of them by any mind. Perhaps a moralist or a poet might call them unsubstantial, because transitory; but in that sense existence itself would be unsubstantial, and all our categories would become confused. Let us reconcile ourselves once for all to transitive existence: the eternal is ours if we truly honour it, but in another sphere; and meantime let us inquire what forms of iteration and of persistence appear in the flux of existence, which is substantial because it flows, and at each moment assaults and betrays our charmed conceptions.

It was well known to the ancients, and is confirmed daily, that when things die they leave heirs: the flies that seem to vanish every winter return every summer. And this pertinacity in substance is not always intermittent; a phase of latency, silent but deeply real, often connects the phases of activity. Sleep and night are not nothing: in them substance most certainly *But in fact nature is full of inheritance, potentiality, and latent phases.* endures, and even gathers strength, or unfolds its hidden coils. Then the spirit, in withdrawing into slumber, seems to return into the womb, into a security and naturalness much deeper than its distracted life. It knows that while it sleeps all things wait, last, and ripen; they all breathe inwardly with that same peace which returns to it only in the night. Those heavenly bodies, which when gaped at seemed but twinkling specks, are in reality sleeping giants; they roll with an enormous momentum at prodigious distances, and keep the world in equilibrium. The rocks are rooted in their buried foundations, the bed of the sea stretches beneath it, and holds it; the earth broods over its ominous substance, like a fiery orange with a rind of stone. It is this universal pause and readiness in things, guarding us unwatched, that chiefly supports our sanity and courage. This constancy gives us security; the eyes may close in peace, while the child's dreaming hand, half closing, prepares to grasp a sword.

The ancients also observed how regularly some objects may be transformed into others, as water into ice or vapour; and that there is a certain equivalence through these phases in their quantity or energy. The seasons return, their fruits varying with the weather; the generations repeat themselves, but mixing their breed; and there is always a potentiality of reversion to a former constellation of properties, prevented only by cross-currents of change. Even where evolution is not cyclical, but creates new forms, it is proportionate and still conservative; anything does not succeed anywhere to anything else. Nothing new arises except out of seeds differently watered, measurably, locally, conditionally. A limited potentiality, an inherited substance, links all the transformations of things together. They pass their matter on to one another; their matter is the principle of their equivalence and continuity. When objects are mutually convertible, they are substantial: were they disembodied essences it would be neither necessary nor intelligible that one should yield to the other in any order, or with any proportion in quantity or quality. But when substantial things perish, we know very well that their elements are simply dispersed, and go to swell the substance of other parts of nature. A long and victorious husbandry has enabled us to trace these migrations of substance; so much so that it has become a plausible hypothesis, countenanced by many an art and many an experiment, that substance is constant in quantity, and never created or destroyed. Only a certain number of loaves can be baked from a barrel of flour; and it would be a miracle if twelve loaves could satisfy the hunger of five thousand people. Famine and war, commerce and prosperity are evident

Substance is quantitative and its changes proportionate and measurable.

phases in this natural economy: friction and crowding of substance here, scarcity there, and everywhere a limited, special, temporary opportunity for existence.

It is to be observed, however, that this quantitative limitation in things is, for human experience and science, rather a matter of averages and of proportion between desultory facts than any traceable persistence in particular substances; genesis is roughly subject to calculation and responsive to custom, but its inner texture eludes observation. Nor is this to be *Substance need not endure after the manner of feelings or images in sense.* wondered at, or set down as an argument against substance altogether: because, if we remember how and why substance is posited in the beginning, we shall not expect it to exhibit the sort of permanence which belongs to specious objects. Specious objects are mere essences; in themselves they are eternal and always recoverable in their absolute identity, except for physical difficulties in reproducing the same attitude in the psyche. Substance, on the contrary, is internally in flux. So that the presumption of identity with which we revert to an essence, or to a term in discourse, is likely to be ill-grounded if we transfer it to a thing, the substance of which is always changing its form. Moreover, the very notion of persistence, like all notions, is a specious essence: it is cumulative and emotional and given in that dumb feeling of duration of which a certain specious philosophy has made so much. It is not to be expected that substance should realise internally this specious quality, which may express in human intuition one aspect of its movement. The feeling of blank duration itself covers a slumbering life in the psyche, roughly sustained and rhythmical, like breathing, but by no means changeless or simple. Obvious persistence is a comment made superficially on a physical flux not clearly discerned; whereas the persistence of substance is something integral to that flux itself, rendering its changes changes, and its phases successive or contiguous.

If the elements of substance resembled persistent images in sense, or were indestructible cubes, spheres, or pyramids, these Egyptian solids would hardly possess the sort of permanence impressing the traveller who stops to admire the Pyramid of Cheops. This pyramid was once built, yet it defies time paradoxically. The stars have the same sublimity, for they ought to burn out or fall from heaven and yet (in our limited experience) they do not: so that an existence seems to us to have put on the eternity of an essence, and by this marvel our own steps and breath and vapid thoughts are rebuked and arrested. But atoms having immutable geometrical forms and no inner substance save pure Being, would be eternal by definition, and not suitable elements of existence at all. They would have no scale for time within them, no sensitiveness to motion or change of relations. Their inner nature would be irrelevant to that flux of existence which it was designed to render intelligible. It would be only their changing arrangement in the void that would determine the field of action. And since the void has pure Being in it no less than an atom (both having geometrical extension for their essence) it is not easy to see how the limits or the position of an atom could themselves be determined. A crumbling pyramid is more substantial than an eternal one.

Pictorial character of geometrical atoms.

Indeed if those Egyptian solids were existing bodies and not merely geometrical essences, their indestructibility, supposing them indestructible, would be a contingent and merely historical fact. It is evident that a spherical, cubical, or pyramidal body *might* at any time fall to pieces; it is an atom provisionally, by courtesy, by virtue of its function in a given mechanism;

If substance takes geometrical forms, it still supports and survives them.

in its existence and substance, which are centred equally in every part, it is thoroughly divisible. Yet, in admitting this undeniable possibility, or rather this natural presumption, that Egyptian atoms should some day crumble, we still posit and imply persistence in the world; for the principle of existence in those fragments would be the same as in the atoms when they were whole, and the same medium of space and time, or whatever else it may be, and the same fatality of motion and of order would permeate that dust and govern its destinies. It was evidently these deeper properties of substance that kept those atoms whole, if perhaps during some cycle of natural existence they remained indestructible; and among those deeper properties we must count the void in which those atoms could move and the mysterious cohesion and fertility of some of their aggregates, by which nature is diversified and made alive.

The atomic theory is, nevertheless, in one sense, inherent in physics, and alone possible; because the very nature of existence is to be dispersed in centres, dislocated, corpuscular, granular; the parts must be particulars externally related. Any demand for a unity not a unity of arrangement, derivation, or conjunction turns its back on existence. Indeed these very unities of arrangement, when substance realises them, are not contained in the substance at any point, or at any moment; they are not seated, for instance, in any intuition which may define them or in any perception which may posit them in the world. They belong, if they are realised, to the realm of truth. It is simply true that the parts of substance have assumed that arrangement; and this truth is not proved by the mere intuition of such a unity, which might be specious only, but must be made the goal of a laborious investigation and a practical faith. The seen unities are not

Yet substance is atomic in as much as existence is discrete; and all enveloping unities are only truths about it.

false; they are manifestations of substance like the intuitions which we have when we read poetry; but they express our reaction to a manifold object and our gross relation to it, rather than the diffuse substance of that object itself. The unities and arrangements embodied in substance are not separable from it or from its flux; and like substance and its flux these can be known only functionally.

For this reason an atomism which professes to *define* its atoms trespasses against the modesty of our genuine contacts with things. The atomism of Democritus, with the Cartesian notion of sub-
stance and the Newtonian notion of space,
time, and matter, are all too graphic and mathematical;
they betray their Eleatic and Pythagorean origin; they
share a poetic or mythological gnosticism which thinks
to decipher the heart of nature in terms of human
intuition. These terms may be admirably chosen and
the best possible; but their value is not exhaustive and
must always remain symbolical. The persistence of
substance can hardly be intrinsically similar to the
stubbornness of some ghostly image that will not down.

Illusion of scientific gnosticism.

Great philosophers, having been men of universal
mind, have instinctively set the same standard of
accuracy and truth for all their investigations.
As there is a possibility of literal or intuitive
knowledge in some fields, they have desired
such knowledge everywhere; but in physics,
and in regard to the intrinsic properties of
substance, such knowledge is impossible. Intuition lies at the opposite end of the gamut of nature;
its simplest object covers an immense complexity, a
voluminous heritage, in the animal soul. Where
literal knowledge is possible—apart from contemplation of essence, which is complex feeling rather than
knowledge—is in literary psychology. Here we often
conceive our object exactly as it was or may be: be-

*Intuitive knowledge or divina-
tion is proper only to moral subjects.*

cause it is no more improbable that two brothers should feel and think alike than that two similar leaves should sprout on the same tree. Therefore poetry is, in one sense, truer than science, and more satisfactory to a seasoned and exacting mind. Poetry reveals one sort of truth completely, because reality in that quarter is no more defined or tangible than poetry itself; and it clarifies human experience of other things also, earthly and divine, without falsifying these things more than experience falsifies them already. Science, on the contrary, the deeper it goes, gets thinner and thinner and cheats us altogether, unless we discount its symbols.

We may leave it then for literary psychologists and intuitive metaphysicians to record their experience in ways appealing to men of their own mind; and we may leave it for mathematicians to construct possible worlds. The practical naturalist is concerned only with such properties of substance as are implied, measured, and elicited in his arts and in his explorations. The study of nature is the most picturesque of studies, and full of joy for the innocent mind; but in natural science all is familiarity and nothing comprehension, save as there is a humorous or devout comprehension in foresight and trust.

I may now add to the indispensable properties of substance others which substance seems to possess, and which, since they too are assumed in practice, may be assumed in natural philosophy.

6. *Substance*, in diversifying the field of nature, *sometimes takes the form of animals in whom there are feelings, images, and thoughts. These mental facts are immaterial.* They offer no butt for action and exercise no physical influence on one another.

7. The same *mental facts are manifestations of substance*; in their occurrence they are parts of a total natural event which, on its substantial side, belongs

to the plane of action. They are therefore significant and relevant to action as signs, being
created and controlled by the flux of substance
beneath.

(marginal note) Action, when rational, presupposes that the transformations of substance are continuous, quantitatively constant, and regular in method; and that the spirit, without being a part of that material world, is the consciousness proper to one of the agents there.

8. Beneath the intermittence of phenomena, *the phases or modes through which sub-
substance flows are continuous.*

9. As far as action and calculation can
extend, *the quantity of substance remains equivalent throughout.*

10. *Each phase or mode of substance, although not contained in its antecedents, is predetermined by them in its place and quality,
and proportionate to them in extent and intensity.*
An event will be repeated if ever the constellation of events which bred it should
recur. This regularity in the genesis of modes
or phases of substance is constantly verified
in action on a small scale. To expect it in
substance is the soul of science and art; but
to expect it in phenomena is superstition.

When, then, in perception, action, memory, or hope
experience is treated as significant, a substance is posited

(marginal note) Summary.

which must be external to thought, with its
parts external to one another and each a focus
of existence; a substance which passes through various
phases is unequally distributed in the field of action,
and forms a relative cosmos surrounding each agent.
Action on these assumptions makes it further appear
that this substance is the source of phenomena unsubstantial in themselves but significant of the phases
of substance which produce them; that these phases
are continuous and measurable; and that each transformation, though spontaneous in itself, is repeated
whenever the same conditions recur. Now a substance possessing these functions and these char-
acteristics has a familiar name: it is called matter,

Matter is the medium of calculable art. But I have found from the beginning that the impulse to act and the confidence that the opposite partner in action has specific and measurable resources, are the primary expressions of animal faith; also that animal faith is the only principle by which belief in existence of any kind can be justified or suggested to the spirit. It follows that the only object posited by animal faith is matter; and that all those images which in human experience may be names or signs for objects of belief are, in their ultimate signification, so many names or signs for matter. Their perpetual variety indicates the phases through which the flux of matter is passing in the self, or those which the self is positing in the field of action to which it is responsive. Apart from this material signification, those feelings and perceptions are simply intuitions of essences, essences to which no existence in nature can be assigned. The field of action is accordingly the realm of matter; and I will henceforth call it by that name.

CHAPTER IV

PICTORIAL SPACE AND SENTIMENTAL TIME

THE wise men of Ionia perceived long ago that water, air, or fire, by metamorphosis, might make up the whole life of nature. This is now being rediscovered; but with two interesting differences. Exploration and mathematics have changed the scale of our science: we are acquainted with distance, outwards and inwards. On the other hand, religion and romanticism have established the troubled reign of subjectivity, and have endowed immediate experience with a kind of authority which the maritime Greeks, keen-eyed but practical and argumentative, had never dreamt of. They looked in order to understand and to possess; whereas our philosophy, if not our instinct, reverts with relief from understanding and possession to æsthetic life, as to a surer foundation. Our cosmology has spirited away that living substance which, like Zeus, had many names, but under all of them was felt to be fatally revolving, plastic, and mighty. Air has been attenuated to space, the fluid to motion, fire to light—ambiguous essences which are thought of as existing in nature, and forming its elements, yet are also names for feelings or ghostly concepts floating before the mind; and to these last the modern philosopher, when pressed, is inclined to reduce them.

Why shouldn't some astronomer with one foot in

The genuine physics of the ancients has been extended by mathematics and dislocated by idealism.

idealism tell us that the universe is nothing but light? If we forget that we eat, work, and die, if we forget that we are animals, may we not plausibly think that nothing exists save a certain coloured brightness playing *in vacuo*? And what is con- sciousness, which in the nineteenth century passed for the only reality, but an active and burning light? May not formal science, too, be invoked to prove that light is the only revealer and measurer of the material universe? And yet this light, which should be the source of clearness, is itself the most obscure of things, and its name the most ambiguous of names. For in physics light is understood to be a mysterious agency coursing through space, material in that it has a measurable velocity and does material work, and is a form of vibration or radiation emitted by bodies when ignited, and intercepted and reflected by them even when opaque. It traverses space unceasingly in a thousand directions, leaving it perfectly black and cold. This light is invisible: only gross matter shedding it or catching it can become bright. Plants and blind animals—and even the human eye is blind to some of its rays—may bask in it with profit, being deeply pene- trated by its electric warmth, as by the healing shafts of Apollo.

Typical ambiguity of the word " light ".

To call this cosmic agency light is a poetic metaphor, as if we called it Phœbus; which indeed we might do without absurdity, since Apollo besides his golden locks had his invisible arrows; and these were the dread reality of the god. Only the obvious essence of bright- ness shining in intuition is light proper. This is no insidious power, but an open gift, vouchsafed from moment to moment like daily bread to the spirit; an essence appearing and vanishing as we open or shut the eyes; an intensive quality, æsthetic and emotional, proper to images of colour or visual patterns. It has no velocity or direction or substance or pertinacity;

it is incapable of warming anything or doing any work; it is obvious but cannot be caught, proportionate but not to be measured; remote in its spiritual presence from all the functions of that cosmic fire which, according to Heraclitus, shaped, animated, and devoured everything. Yet this visionary light, which can burn only in the hearth of the soul, lends its name to that mathematical measure of astronomical distances. In one sense, light is the messenger of matter, and carries the eye through time and space almost to infinity, and if we trust its reports dehumanises the universe; but in another sense it tinctures this same universe with a surreptitious humanity, for it seems to reduce everything to immediate experience, to the focus of intuition at any moment in any man; so that both its substance and its measure seem to become æsthetic. Thus the dominance of light, in its two acceptations, marks the two developments, and the fundamental confusion, by which modern cosmology differs from that of the ancients.

That the realm of matter, in its own way, is spatial and temporal follows from the conception of this realm Physical space and time are intrinsic to substance and cannot be defined *a priori*. as the field of action. In action one state of things must pass into another, something must be precipitated, and each direction and each degree of change must be distinguished from all others, which are its alternatives. Substance, if it is to flow and to have parts, must be distributed in centres, each a focus of external and transitional relations with the rest. Interaction and genesis involve this sort of space and time, or create them. But what this physical space or time may properly be, we could know perfectly only by knowing perfectly the intimate movement and ultimate ranges of matter—not a human task. We know matter, as it behoves us to know it, in the measure in which our highly selective action and mental chronicle of action penetrate into its meshes: and presently I shall say something concerning our share in this general flux of existence, and our ways of noting it. Physical space and time are integral elements in this realm of matter: they are *physical*, which is as much as to say that they are contingent, to be explored by experiment rather than by reasoning, to be shared by us rather than contemplated. They may change their form if they choose, like any existence, and may manifest a different essence in their new instances.

It is therefore a problem never to be solved except provisionally and locally, how far a human sensation of sentimental time or of pictorial space, or how far any geometrical model of a pure space or time, may fitly express the temporal and spatial dimensions of nature, or be a true measure for them. Over the field of action, in which we exist, logic, which is but our way of thinking, can have no prior control. Substance did not drop into a world with a previous constitution; it was not obliged to squeeze itself into atoms or to spread itself through infinities, so as to verify the precipitate fancies of future philosophers. To ask whether substance must be discrete or continuous, finite or infinite, many or one, is like asking whether the Almighty must think in French or in English. Having no competence in that sphere, why should we have any preferences? Let physical time and space be infinite or finite, discrete or continuous, unreturning or circular, multiplex or single: these would be curious and impressive truths, if they were discoverable, and too great for ignorant opinion.

Meantime the practical arts retain a great advantage over the speculation which seeks to elucidate them: they deal directly with matter, whereas a graphic or dialectical analysis can be immediately concerned only with images which are symbols, or with symbols which are words. When the act of measuring is an actual transition, like a journey, both the metre and the thing measured are material and equally internal to the flux of substance. The measure is then con-

Physical space and time can be measured only by the material processes that traverse them.

gruous and literal; and the disadvantage of perhaps leaving no precise image in intuition— for what, to intuition, is a pace or a mile?—is counterbalanced by the advantage of bridging truly external relations, and catching nature in her own net. A graphic calculus or a map may afterwards be constructed to give definition and a common denominator to the parts of this past or possible performance, and to display it as a whole to intuition—but now in another realm of being from that in which it might actually occur: for it would occur in the realm of matter, and it is surveyed as an essence. This is not a defect in the survey, but the condition of inspection or retrospect, which is the translation of an event into an idea, and not a repetition of the same event. As literature is but childish exclamation modulated and transcribed, so scientific imagination is but sensation steadied and defined. Instead of the flying miscellany of natural images—vivid but treacherous tokens of what nature is doing—science sets up an idol, simpler and more dignified, but still only an idea.

Mathematical space and time are sublimated essences of this sort. They cannot appear in sense as they are

Mathematical space and time are scientific figments.

defined to be—infinite, equable, and pure; yet they remain specious or ideal in their nature, purified extensions or generalisations of the imagery of sense. It is contact with matter, patient empirical art, that guides this idealisation, so that the Egyptian blocks may be fit and four-square, and the planets may not belie the prophet; and this advance in the validity and precision of the symbols used, in spite of their greater tenuity, causes them to be mistaken, as the crude images of sense were at first, for the very essence of matter. Having erected and polished our mathematical idol, we suppose ourselves to behold intuitively what space and time are physically; we even feel confident that it is impossible for them not to exist, or to exist otherwise. The clearness and necessity native to essence when kept in its own realm are thus attributed to the realm of matter, where all is profound fertility and darkness; and having discarded one or two optical illusions, and straightened out one or two perspectives in religious legend, we feel all the freer to endow the residue of our imaginative baggage with a perfect substantiality.

We might have done better, perhaps, like the animals or the saints, if we had continued to trust instinctively in the secret harmonies of the realm of matter, or of the kingdom of God; we might have lived on, imaginatively, in the world of poetry, which is often pragmatic and hygienic enough. But there are natural stages and shifts in human ideation: every age has its peculiar insights and new illusions. The terms of science, like those of sense, are essences describing in human discourse the objects encountered in action. This relative function removes them, and ought to remove them, from any passive or complete iteration of the realm of matter in its intrinsic essence. When the mathematician applies his calculus to nature, he does so tentatively, after having taken a hint from nature herself, by selecting for his unit some simple image which action and comparison of cases have shown to have prophetic value; and in his most wonderful successes, if he is wise, he keeps his distance and his sense of abstraction. Here lies the legitimate magic of poetic intuitions, such as are these intuitions of time and space; that, being incarnations of spirit on some animal occasion, they have a double affinity, here to spirit and there to matter, and that with the authority proper to their intended object they associate the form

E

and accent of the free symbol which names it. What was only interaction becomes also perception, and what was a process becomes also a drama; and these moral overtones, on their new emotional plane, are the first ideas, the beginnings of knowledge, of their natural occasions.

If we ask how it happens that quite fresh essences, spontaneously evoked in intuition, like sounds or words or mathematical fictions, can nevertheless apply to nature, the answer is not far to seek. Ideas apply to their occasions because they arise out of them, mark them, and are a part of the total natural event which controls their development. Mind is a great symptom of health; it appears at victorious moments, changes with them, and recalls them. Even its confusions and agonies are but conflicts in its domination; it would not be there to die, if harmony had not given it birth. The æsthetic originality of sensations and ideas is therefore an innocent privilege, if their practical connections are knit together harmoniously with the environing flux of events. And, on some plane, they *must* be so knit, because sensations and ideas arise only when living beings are actively adjusting, or secretly readjusting, their powers. If the adjustment to the moving environment were perfect, the essences evoked in thought, whatever notes they might freely strike æsthetically, would apply or work perfectly in practice; for it is not the ideas that work there, but the men in whom the ideas have arisen. Moreover, in applying any idea a man must start from a material centre, his own body, and must use a material scale, since neither centre nor scale can be furnished by logic. Numbering is an action: the essence of a number in intuition preserves the cumulative sense of a repeated touching and discrimination of particular things. Measuring is the act

Simple reason why fiction applies to fact.

Mind is bred in the material movements to which it refers, and is controlled by them.

of superposing one material thing on another What
wonder that the notions arising from such operations
apply to their source, and enable the prophet to cry,
as if inspired, that the Lord has ordered all things
in measure and number and weight? These are the
material categories bred in the mind by mechanical
art, and whatever may be later their ideal elaboration,
their validity in the field of action, which is the only
existing world, remains conventional and pragmatic.
An eye sensitive to physical light would have been
useless to the organism, and incidentally would never
have endowed the spirit with the vision of brightness,
were not light mechanically reflected and diversified
by the earthly bodies on which it falls. Signals coming
to the eye would not otherwise be prophetic of rougher
contacts. Nor would pictorial space otherwise have
become what it is for human intelligence, an accurate
and detailed map, drawn according to a private projection, and covering the field of action, or the home-
world of mankind. In consequence, when the sun
rises, it not merely warms the backs of mankind, as
if they were lizards, but it clears away from the spirit
half the terrors of a precarious life. It suddenly extends
the field of grovelling search and opportunity to the
horizon. The gift of specious light, great as it is
æsthetically, would have seemed trivial to the heart,
but for this quicker adjustment to matter and this new
safety expressed in it. Since physical light is an instrument of reaction at long range, specious light, its moral
echo, has become almost a synonym for intelligence.

A chief characteristic of pictorial space, *Pictorial*
which betrays its animal origin, is that it has *space al-*
a centre. This centre is transcendental; that *ways has a tran-*
is to say, it is not determined by any distinc- *scendental*
tion in the parts of space itself, as conceived, *centre in some animal*
all of which are equally central. The dignity *spirit.*
of being a centre comes to any point of space from

the spirit, which some fatality has lodged there, to the exclusion, at least in its own view, of all other places. These other places appear in that view as removed, and ranged in concentric spheres at greater and greater distances. The cosmos of Ptolemy is the perfect model or systematisation of pictorial space. The choice of the earth for a centre, although arbitrary geometrically, was not arbitrary historically, because Ptolemy and all other human beings found themselves on the earth, and were natives of it. So the fatality which always lodges spirit at some one point in nature, and makes this its centre, is not arbitrary biologically: for wherever there is a living organism it becomes a centre for dramatic action and reaction, and thereby calls down spirit to assume that station, and make it a moving vehicle for one phase of its earthly fortunes. Pictorial space therefore reappears, wherever an animal rises to intuition of his environment, and in each case it has its moral or transcendental centre in that animal; a centre which, being transcendental or moral, moves wherever the animal moves, and is repeated without physical contradiction or rivalry in as many places as are ever inhabited by a watchful animal soul.

The name of this relative centre is *here*. Nature, if it has limits and is all measurable by a single measure (which may be doubted), may have a centre, but not in the same sense as pictorial space; for *here*, in pictorial space, is a centre of occupied position and actual reference, the determinant of far and near, forward and back, up and down, right and left: animal categories imposed on the field of action by action itself, and impossible except in a perspective created by living intently in the act of looking, moving, or reaching out from an occupied centre in a particular direction. This direction could not be chosen, or even conceived, except in sympathy with some organic impulse; in pictorial space all structures and lines of cleavage crystallise about the axis of attention. The centre of the cosmos, on the contrary, if it exists, would be determined by reciprocal material relations between its parts; and the choice of a starting-point in surveying it never would shift that centre, but only lead to it, as if to Rome, by a particular road.

When an image of one's own body is included in pictorial space, as happens almost always in action, this image will roughly correspond with the centre of that action in physical space: vision will be centred in the moving hero, and will follow him in his adventures. For even if nature as a whole has no centre, every organism is a focus for its external and changing relations to the rest of the world, and is the centre of a dynamic cosmos relative to itself. Thus pictorial space, spreading round its transcendental point of origin in the attentive spirit, affords a suitable index to that field of action which is its professed object, since the segment of nature implicated in that action actually surrounds and recedes from that action very much as pictorial objects surround the image of the body, and seem to recede from it. In perception, as in painting, distortion is often the secret of significance. Pictorial space achieves something which might have seemed a miracle to a spirit acquainted with matter from the outside, but ignorant of the animal mind, which is the self-consciousness of matter; for pictorial space infuses into its object, physical space, an intrinsic reference to the station, the impulses, and the organs of the creatures ranging within it. This symbolic virtue hangs together with the transcendental status and graphic unity of pictorial space, by virtue of which it forms no part of physical space, but is a new whole symbol for it as a whole. The two belong to different realms of being, like Lucifer and the morning star, that yet bear the same name; and they are connected, not by

The subjective or practical here *travels with the sensitive organism.*

interfering with or patching one another, but by a spontaneous concomitance and mutual implication, so that to find the one, under certain conditions, is to announce the other. Matter, or physical space, at certain nodes in its organisation, grounds and justifies the biassed sensitiveness of animals to their environment; and this biassed sensitiveness, raised to intuition, forms an ocular-muscular perception of that very space; for the intuitions of animals, at least in action, are not pure or contemplative, but by force of the intent involved in action, signify to the spirit the conditions of its existence—in this case the movement and filling of physical space in that neighbourhood.

Sometimes, as in deep thought, no image of one's own body figures at all in intuition. *Here* then means whatever point in imagined space is the centre of attention. *Here* may be the word on the page which I have reached in reading; or if my attention has passed from the words to the images awakened by them in my fancy, *here* may be Dante's Purgatorio, rising solitary out of a glassy sea and lifting its clear-cut terraces in perfect circles, up to the fragrant wood at the summit, whence souls grown too pure for a mild happiness pass into the flame of heaven. *Here* is then at the antipodes of Jerusalem and Calvary; half-way up from the centre of the Earth, which is the Inferno, to the lowest of those concentric celestial spheres, each broader and more luminous, which, as Plotinus would say, are *There*. For, in my contemplative mood, I should be regarding myself as directed away from the earth, and from the Hell in it, and in my pictorial space the Eternal would seem to be the Beyond. But now, perhaps, someone knocks at my door and disturbs my reverie. *Here* is now, if still a purgatory, a purgatory of a very different sort; it is this room in this town where my body finds itself. I look out of the window, and now *here* is Paris;

The objective or contemplative here *travels with the object of attention.*

I notice on my table Baedeker's guide-books and the *Indicateur des chemins de fer*, and I consider how easily *here* may be transferred to quite another geographical place. As to the *here* of a moment ago, it is not only not here, but it is nowhere. It belongs to Dante's imaginary world. It is a theme from the symphony of essence.

The bond between pictorial space and physical space lies in the organ of intuition, which is a part of the agent in action. As this organ extends its instrumental uses, adjusting the organism at long range to its environment in physical space, so and in the same measure this same organ exercises its expressive or spiritual function, and creates a pictorial space for the spirit of that animal. This intuition is an important element in the total consciousness which that spirit can have of its destiny; it *The range and objective centres of pictorial space express the scope of its organ in its reaction on other parts of nature.* sets the stage in which the image of its body is found always occupying the centre, and marks the vital distinctions of forward and back, up and down, far and near. Such relations, though obviously relative to an animal life, are not intransitive, as if they were the baseless invention of some impenetrable atom coming to life; they express a movement. Indeed, it is hardly conceivable that a point or an arrested structure should feel or think. The organ of intuition is rather so much of nature as is engaged in that movement, and contributes to the choice of the essence which that intuition evokes. It might even be said that the whole universe is the ultimate organ of every intuition, as it is the ultimate object of every belief: but the measure in which this is true is most unequal. All intuitions, and especially that of space, take the point of view of some particular creature at some particular juncture; and if we wish to discover the special organ of an intuition, we may do so by internal evidence, noting the moral centre of the given scene, and its pictorial circumference, as we might those of a novel. The novel (unless it is an intentional travesty) will describe the country and age in which it was written; so the intuition will normally describe, and will always betray, that centre of vital relations which is its seat and its author. Thus the degree in which the intuition transcends or ignores that centre, becoming possibly an intuition of pure truth, will mark the degree in which its organ, though particular, is sensitive to the rest of nature.

Besides a specious centre, *here*, pictorial space has a specious scale: it contains a direct emotional sense

The emotional infinite.

of the large and small, the far and near. Size and distance are indeed so emotional that they are more than spatial, and touch the sphere of sentimental time: the " far " is redolent of the prolonged and dubious adventure of reaching it, and the " large " taxes the synthetic power of the eye, or the clasp of the extended arms. Pictorial space itself, especially when empty and considered absolutely, is the very model of vastness; it opens in all directions (something baffling to a hunting animal) and recedes to immeasurable distances. In its presence the breast expands, which is glorious, but the will halts, which is annihilating, and brings tears to the eyes. Therefore the oppressed souls of heroes sighed in Homer, looking into the broad heaven. The notion of the romantic infinite is a sublimation of this helplessness in applying a homely measure to unhomely things; from the practically inexhaustible we pass to the ideally immeasurable or infinite, and find it at once alluring and maddening, inevitable and dubious. Romanticism could not gloat on a more congenial abyss.

The mystery of this mock infinite comes of importing into an essence, mathematically quite definite, the emotions of an explorer. The innumerable would present no difficulty if nobody was condemned to enumerate it;

and nobody is. If nature is in some sense infinite, there will be substance found to occupy all its parts, and establish their real relations: but the geo- metrical model of an infinite empty space is only a phantasm visiting the imagination, pic- torial space washed clean. Having no scale, no separable parts, and none but internal necessary relations, it is an essence without existence. Taken in this capacity it is a per- fectly clear and coherent object: a fact which confirms its specious character and derivation

The mathe- matical infinite is a clear essence, which nature suggests to the mind, appropriate but not substantial.

from a sensuous image; because if it were the essence of matter, as Descartes deputed it to be, it would hardly be clear or distinct to human apprehension. For matter, with all existence supported by matter, is unin- telligible, if for no other reason, because it changes. The light of spirit which shines in the darkness cannot see the primeval darkness which begat it and which it dispels; but in so far as its strength avails it consumes that darkness, as it were, for fuel, and sees that which was dark before by the light which it spreads over it. In this way first pictorial space and then geometrical space are cast like a search-light or a net over the field of action, to map and to measure it; but the principle of action, matter in its native unison and flux, escapes intuition, and may be mapped and measured only ex- ternally, even if quite correctly and safely. This is possible because the darkness of matter is not chaotic or malicious; it does not circumvent the light which plays upon it, but only ignores it, and lets it play on. That light is its own child, its own effluence. The harmony between the depths and the surface, the seed and the flower, is as natural as their diversity.

Pictorial spaces are pictorial in various degrees: they range from the simplest essence of extensity, through all images of motion, collapse, swiftness, or scenic con- fusion; or they may culminate in a reposeful landscape, and in that essence of empty volume or immensity which, save for the absence of analysis, would fuse with the notion of geometrical space. Perfectly obvious, but not at all geometrical, is the space revealed by internal sensations, when in one's insides something is felt moving, it would be hard to say what, where, or in how many dimensions. In dizziness and dreams there are lapsing pictorial spaces; in semi-consciousness there are un-mapped unrelated spaces waxing and vanishing. It is not only the latitude and longitude of visionary places that are unassignable, but their spatial quality that is unearthly: the talk about flat-land and four dimensions is but a thin scientific parody of the uncertainty of animal sense. Even in rational human experience, the living intuition of space is endlessly qualified. There is the scene-painter's space, divided into a few distinct planes in the direction of vision, but vague beyond and non-existent behind the observer's back. At the theatre the house is not in the same space as the play-scene, nor in the same time—unless you break the dramatic spell, and substitute the material stage and the paid actors for the poetic world in which you ought to have been living. Even in real life, space for most men stops at the horizon; not sharply, for that would suggest a beyond, but by fancy merely dying out, so that a beyond is not needed, and in fact does not exist in that space. It was in this way that the ancients conceived a round heaven divided into concentric layers, without thinking of the infinity beyond; for the empyrean, when that was invented, was rather an ocean of light than an abyss of nothingness. The views of storks about space —and they must be valid pragmatically—would doubt-less baffle us altogether, and the logic of them might seem to us absurd when translated into our language. Our own topographical knowledge is the fruit of accu-mulation and synthesis, and doubtless truer of nature

Neglected original spaces of sense.

as a whole, though perhaps less penetrating in some dimensions; and its precision renders us intolerant or forgetful of immediate experience even in ourselves. Only in tales or superstitions do we recover at times the elasticity of ignorance, and plunge innocently into as many pictorial spaces as may open out spontaneously before the mind. Even an intelligent man of action will sometimes stop to notice these unauthorised vistas with a humorous affection, as he might play with a child. Yet they may be, in their sporadic way, short cuts to things remote or future, incoherently but vividly reported, like Africa and Norway to the stork; and in any case they are collateral with the elements of our scientific conceptions. Pictures are to knowledge as sound is to language. *Some* true indication is contained in any sensation, since *something* must have happened materially to produce it; but knowledge, synthesis, choice of a centre, and range in apprehension are all adventitious to the existing object: they transfer it from physical to pictorial space, and transpose the parts of it perceived at all into terms of essence.

Pictorial space is one of the dearest possessions of the human spirit: it would be thankless of us to be impatient because it is subjective, as if it ought not to have been so. It might no doubt have had a different sensuous texture, and might have conveyed much the same practical information in that other guise; but it could hardly have been more beautiful than, to the human eye, are the colours of the spectrum, the forms of motion, and the spheres of shadow and of light. If our senses had dogged more faithfully the steps of mutation in matter, we may doubt whether they would have rendered so well the results and scope of those mutations, on the scale of the human body. In science, as in religion, little would be gained by an exchange of idols. Criticism would not be enlightening if it

Pictorial space is beautiful and perhaps transitory.

disgusted us with vision, or led us to quarrel with ideas because they are not things. Ideas are better than things; and one of the happiest fruits of existing in physical space is that pictorial spaces may be based upon it. The wise man is content with his native language: he would not be a better poet or a sharper judge in any other. Pictorial conventions would not have established themselves in the eye or brain if they could not be innocently and harmoniously associated with the business of life; they are to be smilingly welcomed, like strangers coming in the name of the Lord. But the Lord may presently send other messengers: pictorial conventions may vary from age to age and in different races, even if the universe at large is not much changed. Yet this deeper possibility, too, should be remembered by a spirit that would not put all its eggs in one basket: the measure of descriptive truth now possessed by pictorial space need not always belong to it. Its beauty is its own; but if the world fell back into chaos and reconstituted itself differently, our pictorial space would have become obsolete. Other conventions would flourish and other peacocks would spread their tails: all to the greater glory of intuition, so long as intuition survived.

I speak here impulsively of the future; but if the return to chaos were complete, if substance, which is the principle of continuity, were itself destroyed, then there would be no sense in saying that time in the second cosmos was future from the point of view of the first. This firstness and secondness would be reversible, and imputed only because I, from the outside, happened to think of one world before the other. It would be substance in me that alone would actually have passed from the thought of one to the thought of the other, and only my intuition would have connected their essences in a specious

In nature succession is dependent on derivation and mediated by matter.

time. As the space of neither world would lie in the
space of the other, so the histories of the two worlds
would run irrelevant courses, and be neither before
nor after each other, nor simultaneous. For by
physical time I understand an order of derivation integral to the flux of matter; so that if two worlds had
no material connection, and neither was in any of its
parts derived from the other, they could not possibly
have positions in the same physical time. The same
essence of succession might be exhibited in both; the
same kind of temporal vistas might perplex the sentimental inhabitants of each of them; but no date in
one would coincide with a date in the other, nor would
their respective temporal scales and rates of precipitation have any common measure.

The notion that there is and can be but one time,
and that half of it is always intrinsically past and the
other half always intrinsically future, belongs
to the normal pathology of an animal mind: Specious
time, with
it marks the egotistical outlook of an active   its moral
contrast
being endowed with imagination. Such a   between
being will project the moral contrast pro-   past and
future, is
duced by his momentary absorption in action   a vista in
upon the conditions and history of that   the animal
mind.
action, and upon the universe at large. A
perspective of hope and one of reminiscence continually divide for him a specious eternity; and for
him the dramatic centre of existence, though always
at a different point in physical time, will always be
precisely in himself.

Presentness is the coming, lasting, or passing away
of an essence, either in matter or in intuition. This
presentness is a character intrinsic to all   Existence
existence, since an essence would not be   and change
are in-
exemplified in any particular instance unless   trinsically
it came into, or went out of, a medium alien   present.
to it. Such coming and going, with the interval (if

any) between, constitute the exemplification of that essence, either in the realm of matter or in that of spirit. Thus presentness, taken absolutely, is another name for the actuality which every event possesses in its own day, and which gives it its place for ever in the realm of truth. But taken relatively, as it is more natural to take it, presentness is rather a name for the middle position which every moment of existence occupies between its sources and its results. This presentness is pervasive; a moment does not fail to be eternally present because it never was and never can be present at any other moment. This is the ubiquity of actuality, or if you will, of selfishness: because that very leap and cry which brings each moment to birth cuts it off from everything else; the rest becomes, and must for ever remain, external to it. And this division is as requisite as this actuality: the moment does not, as if by some sin or delusion, cut itself off from some placid unitary continuum in which it ought to have remained embedded; it is not a fragment torn from eternity. On the contrary, its place in eternity is established by that severance. It is one wave in a sea that is nothing but waves. That from which it cuts itself off cuts itself off from it in turn, by the same necessity of its being; and every part of that remainder, with the very same leap and cry, cuts itself off from every other part.

Now life is a rich and complex instance of this precipitation and self-assertion, and of this pervasive presentness. Intuition, when it arises, arises within a physical moment, and expresses a passing condition of the psyche. Feelings and thoughts are parts of natural events; they belong to the self which generates them in one of its physical phases. Intuition creates a synthesis in present sensibility; it is an act of attention occurring here and now. It has not, intrinsically,

Intuition shares this physical presentness, but may conceive temporal perspectives.

any miraculous transcendence, as if it spontaneously revealed distant things as they are or were or shall be. Yet in expressing the moment intuition evokes essences; and these essences, coming as they come in the heat of action, and attributed as they are to the objects of physical pursuit or physical attention, may bring tidings of facts at any distance. Within the life of the organism this distance is primarily a distance in physical time—a distance which intuition synthesises in the feeling of duration. For the animal psyche is retentive and wound up to go on; she is full of survivals and preparations. This gathered experience and this potentiality work within her automatically: but sometimes she becomes aware of them in part, in so far as she learns to project given essences and to develop spatial and temporal perspectives within the specious field of the moment.

This feat is made easy by the frequent complexity of the specious field, in which one feature may be seen to vanish or to appear whilst others persist. The essence of change includes a direction in the felt substitution of term for term; it therefore includes the notion of the earlier absence of something now given, and of the earlier presence of something now absent. This is the very sense of existence and of time, and the key to all intelligence and dominion over reality. It contains *the principle* of transitive knowledge, since the present is aware of the past, and I in this condition think of myself in another condition; and it supplies *an instance* of transitive cognition which is knowledge in the sense of being true; because the essence of transition given in intuition is elicited directly by actual partial transitions in the state of the psyche, and this psyche is a congruent part of nature; so that when the essence of transition given now is projected over all physical time, it is plausibly projected and has every chance of being true.

Thus sentimental time is a genuine, if poetical, version of the march of existence, even as pictorial space is a genuine, if poetical, version of its distribution. The views taken are short, especially towards the future, but being extensible they suggest well enough the unfathomable depths of physical time in both directions; and if the views, being views, must be taken from some arbitrary point, they may be exchanged for one another, thus annulling the bias of each, in so far as the others contradict it. I am far from wishing to assert that the remainder or resultant will be the essence of physical time; but for human purposes a just view enough is obtained if we remember that each *now* and *here* is called so only by one voice, and that all other voices call it a *then* and a *there*. It is inevitable, and yet outrageous, that every day and year, every opinion and interest, should think itself alone truly alive and alone basking in the noon of reality. The present is indeed a true focus, an actual consummation, in so far as spirit is awake in it; and it could not have a universal scope if it had not a particular foundation. To uproot intuition from its soil in animal life would be to kill it, or if somehow it were alleged to survive, to render it homeless in the realm of matter. The body is not a prison only, but a watchtower; and the spirit would live in darkness or die of inanition if it could not open the trap-door of action, downwards towards its foundations and food in matter; or if it could not open the two windows of time, eastward and westward, towards rising or sinking constellations. It is no cruel fate, but its own nature, that imprisons life in the moment, and prevents it from taking just cognisance of any other time save by a great effort of intelligence.

If the present could see the past and the future truly, it would not feel its own pre-eminence; it would

A dramatic view of time is natural and proper to an animal spirit.

substitute their intrinsic essences for the essences of their effects within its own compass, or for its anticipations of them. It would thereby cease to be this waking moment in this animal life, and would rise into a preternatural impartiality and ubiquity. For the double aerial perspective in which a living moment sees the future and the past is a false perspective; it paints in evanescent colours what is in fact a steady procession of realities, all equally vivid and complete; it renders the past faded and dead, and the future uncertain and non-existent. But this is egregious egotism and animal blindness. The past is not faded, except in the eye of the present, and the future is not ambiguous, except to ignorant conjecture. Yet it is only by conjecture or confused reminiscence that the present is able to conceive them. The present had to choose between misrepresentation and blindness: for if it had not seen the past and future in a selfish perspective, it could not have been aware of them at all. In the romantic guise of what is not yet or what is no longer, the fleeting moment is able to recognise outlying existences, and to indicate to its own spirit the direction in which they lie. Flux, by its very essence, cannot be synthesised; it must be undergone. The animal egotism which gives it a centre now and not then, contrary to fact, yet enables the passage from then to now, and from now onwards to another now, to be given in a dramatic synthesis—a synthesis which actual succession excludes. But without synthesis there is no intuition, no feeling: so that the sentimental perspectives of time are the only available forms in which a physical flux could be reported to the spirit.

The least sentimental term in sentimental time is the term *now*, because it marks the junction of fancy with action. *Now* is often a word of command; it

Its error is due to relativity, and relativity is necessary to its existence.

F

leans towards the future, and seems to be the voice of the present summoning the next moment to arise, and pouncing upon it when it does so. For *now* has in it emotionally all the cheeriness of material change: it comes out of the past as if impatient at not having come sooner, and it passes into the future with alacrity, as if confident of losing nothing by moving on. For it is evident that actual succession can contain nothing but *nows*, so that *now* in a certain way is immortal. But this immortality is only a continual reiteration, a series of moments each without self-possession and without assurance of any other moment; so that if ever the *now* loses its indicative practical force and becomes introspective, it becomes acutely sentimental, a perpetual hope unrealised and a perpetual dying.

The joyous *now*.

Various other modes of felt time cluster round this travelling *now*. *Just now*, for instance, is already retrospective, and marks a condition of things no longer quite in hand, already an object of intent and of questionable knowledge, yet still so near, that any mistake about it would be more like an illusion of sense than like a false assertion. *Just now* is like a spoken word lingering in the ear, so distinctly that what it was may still be observed, and described by inspection; and yet the description arising is distinguishable from it, and the two may be compared within the field of intuition. For though the voice is silent, I am still able to hear it inwardly; and its increasing uncertainty, its evanescence, is a notable part of what I perceive. At last the reverberation becomes inaudible, and I have only an image formed at intervals by silently repeating the word. If I am able to repeat it, it is not because I can mentally remember it, but I remember it mentally because I am able to repeat it physically. This muted repetition is thereafter my physical

The foreground of absent time.

memory of what that sound was at its loudest; it suggests the glorious *then*, contrasted with this silent and empty *now*.

The psyche is full of potential experience—pictures which she is ready to paint and would wish to hang—but the question is where, in those vast vague Its middle galleries of fancied time, she shall hang them. distance. When the picture is composed and, so to speak, in her hand, but she can find no hook for it in the direction of action, she says *not yet*; and unless she drops and forgets it, she may go on to say *soon*, or *some day*; or if, diabolically, the place it was about to occupy appears otherwise filled, she may cry, *too late*. There are corresponding removes and vacillations in the direction of the past, where active impulses are not engaged. A risen image looks for points of attachment in the realm of truth; the sentimental mind would hardly entertain it, unless it could pass for somebody's ghost. A place can be found for almost anything in the fog of distance, and the most miraculous tale begins with *once upon a time*. There is hardly more definiteness, with added melancholy, in saying *long ago*. The event has sunk, for sentiment, below the horizon, into the night where everything sleeps which, though theoretically credited, is not relevant to present action.

All, however, is not flaccidity and weakness in sentimental time; it has its noble notes in the sublime *always* and the tragic *never*. These terms, Imaginary when true, describe facts in physical time, tragic and their force comes from that backing, but survey of it in its not their sentimental colour; for there is entirety. nothing tragic in the mere absence of anything from the universe, and nothing sublime in the presence there of such elements as may happen to be pervasive, like matter and change. The sublimity or tragedy comes from projecting sentimental time, with its human centre, upon the canvas of nature. *Never* then proclaims an ultimate despair or relief. It professes to banish from the whole past or future some essence now vividly present to the mind, tempting or horrible; and the living roots of that possibility here in the soul render the denial of it in nature violent and marvellous. That something arresting to thought should be absent from the field of action causes a cruel division in the animal spirit; for this spirit can live only by grace of material circumstances, yet, being a spirit, it can live only by distinguishing eternal essences. Its joy lies in being perpetually promoted to intuition and confirmed in it; but it is distracted if its intuitions are thwarted, and expel or contradict one another. Therefore, whenever the spirit finds some steadfast feature in the world, it breathes, even in the midst of action and discovery, its native air. That which exists always, even if only a type or a law, seems almost raised above existence: *always* assimilates time to eternity. Imagination then flatters itself that it dominates the universe, as it was in the beginning, is now, and ever shall be. In fact, imagination can never synthesise anything but its own vistas, in a specious, not a physical time; but, if the vista had happened to be true, and if physical time had repeated endlessly the feature now singly conceived, thought would have marvellously domesticated that crawling monster, prescribing, or seeming to prescribe, how and how far it should uncoil itself. In respect to the whole flux of existence such a boast is gratuitous; but it may be justified in respect to that field of action on which the spirit immediately depends.

Spirit, however scattered its occasions and instances may be, is always synthetic in its intellectual energy or actuality: it gives the form of totality to its world. The frontiers may be vague and the features confused, but they could not be confused or vague if they were not features and frontiers

The specious present.

of a single scene. Synthesis is a prerequisite to the
sensation of change. An image of motion or a feeling
of lapse is a single feeling and a single image. That
exciting experience in which *now*, *now*, keeps ringing
like a bell would not be a strained experience of the
mind, nor more than so many fresh experiences, if the
iteration were not synthesised, each stroke being received by a sensorium already alive, and as it were
elastic, so that the dying strokes and others imminent
formed with the fresh stroke a single temporal landscape,
a wide indefinite *now* open to intuition, which psychologists call the specious present. This intuition no doubt
has its basis in the datable physical moment, in a
definite phase of the organism; but the temporal landscape given in it is ideal, and has no date and no clear
limits; indeed, it is a miniature of all time, as imagination might survey and picture it. A few more details
on the same canvas, a closer attention to the remoter
vistas, and this specious present might contain all
knowledge. All that the most learned historian or
the deepest theologian has ever actually conceived must
have come to him in the specious present. Unless
action concentrates the attention on the forward edge
of this prospect, on the budding *now*, the whole leans
rather towards the past, and grows more and more
extended. It becomes full of things vain for our
present purpose. Even when action or scientific
observation rescue the specious present from this
sentimentality, they leave it ideal, and its field a purely
sensuous unit.

Action and scientific observation, though framed
within the specious present in perception, ignore it in
practice; but arts like music and eloquence Its possible
are directed (without knowing it) to enriching richness,
this specious present and rendering it, in emotional and
some climax, so overwhelmingly pregnant æsthetic.
and brilliant, that scientific observation and action

become impossible; as if the flux of things had cul-
minated, collected all its treasures, and wished, at least
for a moment, to stop and possess them.   Under such
tension, when the spirit takes flight towards its proper
objects, essence and truth, the body, which cannot
follow, bursts into irrelevant action, such as tears or
applause or laughter or contortions.   Synthesis, which
must be material before it can be spiritual, has then
brought to a head more currents than can flow into
any useful channel, and some random outlet must be
found for that physical fullness and that physical impotence.   Meantime intuition shines in all its glory.
On lesser occasions, when attention lights up some
particular path in the field of action, spirit, being all
eagerness and appetition, almost seems to be a form of
energy or source of motion in matter.   But the fact
that it is always wholly contemplative becomes evident
in its richer moments; for then the specious present
extends far beyond the urgent occasion for action, and
may even drop its conscious relevance to the person
or the hour; and at the same time its vistas will cease
to be sentimental, because the survey of them will have
become intellectual and impartially receptive.

The specious present is dateless, but it is temporal;[1]
it is the vaguely limited foreground of sentimental
time.   In it the precipitation proper to existence, the ticking of the great clock is
clearly audible: the bodily feeling of the
moment is complicated in it by after-images
of instants receding, and strained by antici-
pation of instants to come.   As the psyche
can synthesise in memory the fading impressions
that reverberate within her, so she can prefigure and
rehearse the acts for which she is making ready.   A
pleasant rumble and a large assurance thus pervade

Flux, synthesised in the specious present, yields the perception of flux.

----

[1] For the exact force of these terms, see *Scepticism and Animal Faith*, p. 270.

animal consciousness in its calmer moments. There is no knife-edge here of present time, nor any exact frontiers, but a virtual possession of the past and even of the future; because the psyche is magnificently confident not only that a future will be forthcoming, but that its paces will be familiar, and easy to deal with; in fact she is quietly putting irons in the fire, and means to have a hand in shaping it. The general character of the future is felt to be as sure as the ebb and flow of the tide, or as the rest of a sentence half spoken; and this assurance, which might seem groundless, is not so, because the psyche is not a detached spirit, examining the world by the light of some absolute logic. She is herself a material engine, a part of that substantial flux which exists only by bridging its intervals, and is defined as much by what it becomes as by what it may have been. That future which is in part her product is, in that measure, her substance transformed, or by its action transforming the surrounding substance.

At bottom, then, the future is no new event, but the rest of this transformation. In an organism like the psyche, it is the present pregnancy of matter that determines the further develop- ment of its forms. Of course this develop- ment may be cut short at any point by contacts with other organisms, or with the inorganic; and then, if the psyche survives, she will be diverted in some new direction, at first violent and unpredictable. But if she could understand fully all the substance of which she is a portion, she would dominate in the specious present the remotest future of her universe, as well as its deepest past; for physical time is nothing but the deployment of substance, and the essence of this substance is the form which, if free, it would realise in its deployment. The psyche, then, is not radically deceived in her somnolent confidence in the future, nor in her conviction

The involution of events in the psyche renders her capable of true memory and prophecy.

that she helps to determine it. The future may be largely foreseen, or brought about as intended, even as the past may be largely remembered; the psyche has materials within the moment for both those temporal vistas. It is her egotism here that is in error rather than her faith; for the vivacity of her wishes or momentary fancies may obscure her sense for things at a distance; and beyond the chance limits of the specious present, she may think the future indeterminate and unreal, and the past dead.

The dead past? Certainly all years prior to A.D. 1920 are past at the time when I write these words, and all later years are future, and to me uncertain; yet the reader knows that one of the years perhaps long subsequent to 1920 is as living and sure as 1920 is to me now. My problematic future will be his living present, and both presently a third man's irrevocable past. There is no moment in the whole course of nature (unless there be a first and a last moment) which is not both future and past for an infinity of other moments. In itself, by virtue of its emergence in a world of change, each moment is unstably present, or in the act of elapsing; and by virtue of its position in the order of generation, both pastness and futurity pervade it eternally. Such double abysmal absence is the price which existence pays for its momentary emphasis. Futurity and pastness, the reproach of being not yet and being no longer, fall upon it from different quarters, like lights of different colours; and these same colours, like the red light and the green light of a ship, it itself carries and spreads in opposite directions. And these shafts cross one another with a sort of correspondence in contradiction: the moments which any moment calls past call it future, and those which it calls future call it past.

Contradictory epithets of this sort are compatible

Cross-lights of pastness and futurity.

when they are seen to be relative; but it must be understood that they are the relative aspects of something which has an absolute nature of its own, to *Events can be truly* be the foundation of those relations. And *past or* the absolute nature of moments is to be *future only* present: a moment which was not present in *relatively,* itself could not be truly past or future in *and in case they are in-* relation to other moments. What I call the *trinsically present.* past and what I call the future are truly past or future *from here*; but if they were *only* past or *only* future, it would be an egregious error on my part to believe that they were past or future at all, for they would exist only in my present memory or expectation. In their pastness and futurity they would be merely specious, and they would be nothing but parts of a present image. If I pretended that they recalled or forecast anything, I should be deceived; for nothing of that kind, either in the past or in the future, would ever rejoice in presentness and exist on its own account. Thus only false memory and false expectation end in events intrinsically past or intrinsically future—that is to say, intrinsically sentimental. False legends and false hopes indeed have their being only in perspective; their only substance is the thought of them now, and it is only as absent that they are ever present.

Romantic idealism, which saturates modern speculation even when not avowed, if it were not halting and ambiguous, would reduce all time to the *Sentimental* picture of time, and establish the solipsism *time is the* of the present moment. And the present *only time recognised* moment indeed includes and absorbs all senti- *by modern* mental time: apart from its vistas, neither *idealism.* the past nor the future would be at all romantic or unreal. Common sense admits this in respect to the past. The equal reality of the past with the present, and its fixity of essence, so that ideas of it may be false or true, are not seriously questioned. But in respect to the future, imagination is less respectful of fact, and flounders in an abyss to which it attributes its own vagueness. The prevision which the psyche often has of its future actions, as in planning or calculation, ought to give steadiness to thoughts of the future, in as much as here the causes of future events are already found at work; and the ancients, who were not sentimental, cultivated policy and prophecy, endeavouring to define the future through its signs and causes, as we define the past through its memorials. But modern anticipations are based rather on supposed " laws ", or on intuition of divine purposes; that is, on forms found in the perspective of events, as synthesised in imagination: whereby physical time is asked to march to the music which sentimental time may pipe for it.

In reality, nature moves in a time of her own, everywhere equally present, of which sentimental time is a momentary echo; for sometimes a single pulse of substance may become conscious of its motion, and may fantastically endeavour to embrace the true past and the true future, necessarily external to it, in a single view. This sentimental agony fancy then transfers from its own flutterings to the brisk precipitation and the large somnolence of the general flux, which is neither regretful nor perturbed, and not intent on prolonging one of its phases rather than another. Animal life itself shares this conformity with the flux of things, whenever animal life is perfect; and even perfect intuition shares it, by entirely transmuting motion into light: so that both in rude health and in pure contemplation it either forgets the past and the future altogether, or ceases to be sentimental about them, and learns to feel their direct and native reality, as they feel it themselves.

But the healthy mind transcends it, both in living and in thinking.

CHAPTER V

THE FLUX OF EXISTENCE

SINCE all moments of physical time are intrinsically present, it might seem that real existence was not changeful at all but only, perhaps, asymmet- Hypothesis rical, like a fricze of sculptured arrows all of a static pointing one way, or a file of halted soldiers which the lifting one foot for ever, as if they had meant sense of to march. The illusion of successive events would be would be produced by the eye glancing along an illusion. the frieze or the reviewing officer passing down the line. This ancient persuasion is founded on much moral reflexion and is appropriate to the intellect composing and recomposing its views of the truth. The realm of truth is indeed eternal and static, and the exploring spirit may traverse it by one or another narrow path in a thousand directions without adding, removing, or changing a single feature of that inde-structible labyrinth. But in regard to the realm of existence this suggestion is inapplicable and radically perverse. Indeed, even on this hypothesis, flux would not be abolished but only transferred from the panorama of facts to the living spirit which, in gradually dis-covering them, would be really passing through a succession of different states. All the questions con-cerning change, time, and existence would recur in respect to this experience and its temporal order; and the dignity of that eternal truth, arrogating to itself

75

the name of reality, would not help at all to explain our passing illusions, and in comparison with their insistence might itself seem rather shadowy and unimportant.

Moreover, whence should reviewing officers or travelling eyes fetch their mobility, save from that *The illusion* very world which this hypothesis declares *would still* to be static? The gift of progressive obser- *really* *change, and* vation is no homeless miracle, no illusion *this in* without a ground; it is a faculty native and *obedience* *to material* appropriate to animals. It is quite true that *causes.* often a movement of attention produces an experience of change before an object, like an inscription, which is materially static; but then it is not a disembodied spirit that freely surveys that monument and notes its parts *seriatim*; an instinctive or trained movement of the eye imposes a temporal order on the words read. Only haste and lack of circumspection in conceiving what spirit is and how it moves could assign to it the origin of change. On the contrary, while spirit is extraordinarily mobile in its existence, it borrows this mobility from the hair-trigger organisation and unstable equilibrium of its organs, and of the stimulations which excite them incessantly. In its own nature, spirit arrests the flux of things, as best it may, in its intuitions, and turns it into a store of synthetic pictures and symbols, sensuous and intellectual. We may therefore say with more reason that the world imposes movement on a spirit which by its own genius would rather be addressed to the eternal, than say that reality seems successive only to a flighty spirit, turning distractedly the leaves of a book written in eternity. Matter, not spirit, is the seat and principle of the flux. Spirit, being an emanation of this flux, seems indeed a pilgrim wandering and almost lost in the wilderness of essence and in the dark treasure-house of truth; but in respect to the realm of matter, spirit is like a child asking questions and making pause, and often brutally run over and crushed by a rush of changes which it cannot understand.

So true is this that even the vistas of sentimental time, although the spirit creates them in its effort to dominate and synthesise the flux of things, yet trouble it a little and seem disquieting. To intense contemplation, memory and prophecy come forward and become present, and the present itself recedes into a wonderful unreality and becomes truth. Everything stands together, like a thing accomplished. *Spirit endures change but, as far as possible, synthesises it into the truth about it.* Prophets do not predict but see, and cry out, even if the vision be of the last day of creation: Behold, the trump blew, and the heavens fell. Such pictorial prophecy, like pictorial memory, is a state of trance: it takes us out of changing time altogether, as it is the function of spirit to take us, either into the realm of truth, if the memories or prophecies are clairvoyant, or else into the realm of essence, if they are false fancies. Meantime historical events, since they are conventional stretches containing variations, continually lose and continually gain existence, never being complete and comprehensive, as is the truth about them. They cannot be gathered up or understood, even by those who enact them, without being sublimated and congealed into their historical essences and forfeiting their natural flux. The dramatic direction which they may retain in visionary memory, like the visible lack of symmetry in the file of halted soldiers or in the sculptured arrows, suggests a movement to the observer only because it induces him to perform one in his survey; but the direction of this survey is reversible, like a film for the cinema. The asymmetrical forms themselves contain no precipitation; they do not destroy and traverse themselves, or take one another's places. They are only a synthetic model or fossil of change.

Modern philosophers, being contemptuous of essences and without a clear conception of them, usually

Hypothesis of an absolute time in which loose facts take their places.
assume the reality of change and succession without much scrutiny; they do not stop to inquire where and by what juxtaposition the quality abandoned yields to the quality acquired. If we venture to imagine what is probably in their minds, I think we shall come upon something like this: that the flux is composed of states of existence, mental, material, or simply qualitative, each of which is a unit and contains no variation; yet they succeed and replace one another because they arise in an underlying pervasive medium, absolute time, which itself lapses inherently and inevitably at a uniform rate, so that all its moments are already dated, and at a precise remove from one another. When states of mind or matter or neutral phenomena arise, they must therefore arise at one or another of these dated instants. Although each fact is an absolute reality in itself, and with no intrinsic relevance to any other fact, yet any of them may be successive or simultaneous, if they occur at identical or successive moments in that everflowing irreversible time.

This conception of a pure yet physical time, in which events of any sort may arise and take their

Its futility.
places, needs only to be described and inspected for it to dissolve into puzzles. Each of its moments would be exactly like every other: far from measuring a scale of duration, they would collapse into identity. I have already indicated the sensuous origin and specious character of this ghost: it is an after-image of the *sensation* of time. But let me now admit the hypothesis of such an intuitive phantom being substantial, and the prior locus of all existence. Events will now be rendered successive simply by their position in pure time, apart from any inner continuity or derivation of one from another; and the absolute

date of each will be the sole character in it by virtue
of which it may be pronounced the source or the result
of any other. But absolute dates are intrinsically in-
discernible and different only in that one is earlier and
another later; so that concrete events will be arranged
in sequence only by virtue of a character in them which
is absolutely indistinguishable.

Here a subtler suggestion might be made by idealists.
Succession, they might say, is a relation between the
characters of events. As existences, all states
of spirit—and for the idealist no other exist-   Hypothesis
ences are possible—are self-created and, in   that suc-
                                                   cession is
status, eternal; they are fragments of the one   a corre-
                                                   spondence
universal mind; but each may be temporal in   of per-
                                                   spectives
its deliverance or in the picture it unfolds.   among
If we could compare these scattered spiritual   dateless
acts—as the idealist is always doing, although   moments.
on his principles it would be impossible—we should see
correspondences, developments, and contradictions in
their objects. A feature central in one view might be
recognised as the same as a feature quite marginal and
faint in another view: the pictured future there might
be the living present here, and the pictured past here,
in some measure, the present there. Comparing and,
as it were, matching these pictures by their rims, we
might compose a tolerably continuous landscape; and by
identifying the original states of spirit, actually existing
each for itself, with those ideal elements which they
supplied to this panorama—another illegitimate habit of
idealists—we might attribute to those existing   It explains
states the dates of their objects, as these re-   away suc-
                                                   cession and
appear in our own synthesis. Thus we think to   abolishes
cast specious time, like a butterfly-net, over   nature.
spirits freely fluttering and dateless in themselves, which
altogether escape it: they are not rendered successive by
the fact that some of them may repeat the beginning and
some the end of what, in our survey, seems a single story.

It is imperative, then, if we wish to understand existence and the succession of its moments, to disregard any synthesis created in imagination between the essences of these moments, or between what are supposed to have been their essences. Actual succession is a substitution, not a perspective. Now, when this transcendental synthetic glance is discounted, are there other elements left in the experience of change which might serve to describe fitly the nature of a flux actual and physical?

The real flux cannot be synthetised.

Certainly there are such intuitions, else even the most tentative and modest approach to an understanding of nature would be denied us. The feeling of persistence or sheer duration is such an intuition. This feeling is more complex than the insight into the eternity of a given essence, in which there is no drag. It is rather a sense of iteration or failure to lapse in something properly transitory: a strange and questionable arrest where movement is latent or imminent. Such a sense of persistence may become tedious, sublime, or excruciating; it includes an acute tension or sense of existence. It is therefore an admirable expression of the life of nature, emphasising the continuity not without implying the variation. It marks the fact that the flux of existence, although it really never stops, often sustains certain recognisable forms, such as the psyche herself, in a precarious being.

How expressed in the feeling of duration.

The counterpart of continuity, interruption, has the same implication. Total catastrophes in nature might occur; but a wholly new world would not remember or suspect its previous non-existence. The great advance in understanding comes when intuition reveals change in some single respect within a constant object. Doubtless, in strictness, when the world changes in any particular its total essence is renewed, since its balance becomes another; yet the new total essence is—and must be, if

How expressed in felt modifications.

the world is to be consecutive—largely similar to the old one; and this not by a groundless accident or magic law, but because the matter of the earlier phase is inherited by the later. This matter, which alone renders either phase a fact and not a mere essence, carries with it its quantity, its energy, and a progressive redistribution of its parts; so that the very principle of genesis, in lending to each moment of the flux its physical existence, determines the essence which it shall exemplify, and determines it in virtue of the continuity and heredity which must bind moments together materially if they are to be successive chronologically. The same material heritage also determines in what measure or in what detail each successive moment shall differ from the previous one, or how far it shall merely rcpeat it; and it renders the world, throughout its moments, somewhat amenable to addition, subtraction, multiplication, and division.

If it is true that we cannot bathe twice in the same river, because the water has flowed on, it is true also that the same water which was formerly here is now farther down; so that we might bathe in it again if only we ran down the bank with greater celerity than the water. But our second plunge, though into the same water, would be at another point in the stream: and it is this combination of continuity with instability that we indicate when we speak of a river or a flux. The dialectic of continuity— whether it may be analysed into an infinite number of discrete points or into an indefinite number of intervals —was probably not considered by nature before she began to exist: there is therefore no need to consider it in describing existence. Continuity, for the naturalist, is merely a name for the fact that existence is a transmitted burden, something that goes on and is kept up. In the midst of death we are in life; destruction and

Physical continuity, which is not dialectical, includes instability, and physical change includes continuity.

G

change are never so complete at any moment as not to continue the previous reality. If each moment made a wholly fresh beginning it would not be a moment in a flux, but simply one member in an original multitude of beings.

Now, this hereditary nature of existence—each moment being *genitum non factum*—is rudely repre-

Moving sensible units bear witness to these hereditary modes of flux.

sented in intuition by any phenomenon which partly changes and partly seems to remain the same. Common sense hypostatises this intuition, when it traces and recognises persons and things, supposed to remain identical in a maze of changing relations; and science only carries this inevitable hypostasis a step further when it conceives permanent atoms, or permanent laws, sustaining the flux of things and keeping it continuous and intelligible. Such science is conscientious fiction: there are presumably no atoms and no laws separable from the concrete strains and movements of the flux, by which its substance is intimately modified; but this substance being hereditary, each of its moments assumes a form derived from the previous posture of things, and offering to observation innumerable repetitions, calculable changes, and familiar habits: otherwise neither life nor observation could ever have arisen in the midst of chaos to take note of its existence.

Substance, with its intrinsic deployment and heredity, would certainly remain mysterious to us even

Evolution and law are summary views of material derivation.

if we could inspect it at close quarters, because it involves an unintelligible alloy added to whatever essences we might assign to it. As things stand, however, the mystery is darkened by the great difference in scale between the texture of matter and that of human ideas; and when, in mathematics, we pursue and almost seem to attain that inhuman reality, we find ourselves in possession of a perfect method of notation from which everything to be noted has disappeared; and the only truth of our most accurate science turns out to be practical and utterly blind. We must revert, in order to recover our sanity and the subject-matter of our natural science, to crude experience and to the common arts; and here everything is on the human scale. Sunset and sunrise, the obvious repetitions in the generations of men and animals, and in their stock passions, hide movements which in nature are probably knit unbrokenly together, and never quite alike, or obedient to any disembodied law. Seen on the human scale, repetitions are perfectly inexplicable: they suggest to the gaping mind a magical control of events by a monotonous destiny: they suggest superstition. But beneath these trite measures, which human wit casts over things, like a net of proverbs, the natural flux goes its own pace, uncontrolled by any magic or logic. It is *natural*: it passes everywhere from what it was at that point, as the conjunction of elements there prompts it to do, never asking whether that conjunction is new or habitual. It knows no desire for novelty, no obsession by rule; it is as willing to run into repetitions as into catastrophes, and it is as likely to suggest to gross observation a law in one place as a purpose in another. Its order in one place may produce a mind to which its general order seems a chaos.

Physical time is another name for this native instability of matter, which, since it has distinct stations or phases, may be observed by spirit, and since it falls into recurring rhythms may be measured by its own stride. These stages and rhythms are essences; and it is in terms of essence that any possible physics is condemned to describe nature; but the description becomes true in so far as these or equivalent essences are actually embodied in the field of action. It is only by such embodiment in matter that essences

The flux of matter first lends existence to such essences as may define it.

can be loosened, as it were, from their essential setting and turned into the characters of facts; or rather—since their essential setting is eternal and holds them even while embodiments of them are passing through existence—it is only by being distributed in the field of action that essences can add for a moment external and variable relations to those which their proper nature involves.

This descent or incarnation of essences cannot be their own doing, since all essences are inert and non-existent. Even in a dream the objects that impose themselves successively on the spirit, being purely imaginary, have no power to maintain themselves or to generate one another, any more than one word or note in the air has the power, in the absence of a vocal instrument, to breed the next word or the next note. It is the slumbering material psyche that generates those feelings and images out of her disquiet, as when awake she generates those words or notes out of her material exuberance; were it not for her stored troubles no insane anxieties or absurd vicissitudes would disturb her sleep. Even the thinnest creations of spirit, therefore, are products of the realm of matter, and possible only within it. Incarnation is no voluntary emanation from above; it is a dire event, a budding torment, here below. A world of accidents, arbitrary and treacherous, first lends to the eternal a temporal existence and a place in the flux.

Particularity and transition are inherent in this nether form of being. Everything that arises is liable to lapse; everything that exists exists by conjunction with other things on its own plane; it belongs somewhere and to a certain time by virtue of the external relations which pin it there. From this an important consequence follows: Existence can have no general or stable medium deeper than itself, such as an absolute space or time through

The flux flows through no prior medium.

which it should flow and which in some respects would control its formation. The flux is itself absolute and the seat of existence: the substance which flows through things cannot exist between them. It bestows on them their hereditary qualities and quantities, and their place in nature. Without substance each phenomenon would be an insulated essence, lacking all force or movement, either internal or transcendent, and incapable of existing in itself or of imposing itself at any particular moment on any particular mind. But the counterpart is no less true: without those exchangeable forms, without running through those distinct states and positions, substance in turn would fade into an essence. Far from being the natural parent of all scattered particular facts, it would be the impotent possibility of their forms only. It would not be that pregnant and labouring matter which fills the world, but the essence at the opposite end of the ontological scale, pure Being, in which all essences are indeed contained, as it were, in solution, but in which none is suffered to come forward with an irrational emphasis, and impudently to exist. In order to exist substance itself must be something in particular, exclusive at each point of what it is at all others.

Having no prior conditions, existence at each node or centre is what it happens to be, showing such a form, energy, intensity, or consciousness as it happens to show. We must consider and inspect each part separately, by transporting ourselves into it at least ideally, before we can say what that part is intrinsically, or how many parts there are, or what is their order. Relations the facts must indeed have, if they are many: first, the relations eternally contrasting their several essences; and secondly, those accidental and variable relations which render these facts existing instances of their essences, and parts of one fluid world. All the axioms of philosophers declaring the world to be necessarily infinite or everlasting

It may take any course and contain any events whatsoever.

or rational or conscious must be received as applying only to their respective systems: the world meantime is just what it is, has been what it has been, and will be what it will be.

Yet, while the character of each fact is self-declared, its place among other facts (such as our belief in it) depends on contacts and transitions between it and the rest of its world. Did it not come from something different and did it not empty itself into something else, it would not contain within itself that stress, that incompleteness, that pervasive mortality, which precisely mark it as actual and living, and both more and less than a pure essence.

Yet in being realised every essence must acquire natural relations.

If each moment of existence is a centre, and self-assertive, it is so by being a focus of rays gathered into it from external sources and discharged again into eventual effects. By virtue of these connections and transmissions its place is fixed in the flux, and it vindicates its right to be called existent, since it is discoverable, measurable, and dated. All that it possesses besides—its intrinsic essence, its originality, its feeling, if it has feeling—is hidden from the world, escapes physics altogether, and merely marks its degree of inspiration: I mean, how much of the eternal it has managed, in passing, to draw down into itself, to illustrate, or to discover.

How express in human language (all the terms of which, unless they are proper names, designate essences) this mixture of self-assertion and instability proper to any moment of existence? The classic expedient is to analyse existence into matter and form, the matter being transmissible and serving to connect moment with moment and to render the later the offspring of the earlier, while the form serves to characterise each moment and give it individuality

Though all existing matter has form it is condemned endlessly to pass from one form to another.

and limits. This is a correct and—as might be seen by reviewing the alternatives—an inevitable way of expressing the nature of change in rhetorical terms. To the senses, to the passions, to the defining intellect the flux of existence is indeed a flight of eternal essences across a permanent screen, in which alone they have their momentary existence—a screen which sometimes seems to be the vague universe and sometimes one's own soul. Yet these categories, being logical or poetical, are not important to the naturalist. No doubt the naturalist too may speak of forms and of matter; but his forms are aggregates, themselves arising and breaking up; and his matter is something existent, the matter actually transmitted and transmuted by nutrition, generation, or labour. This matter everywhere has a particular quality, structure, and potency; and it not only possesses form, as a geometrical solid possesses it, but it is informed with the peculiar essence of existence also, which includes inner instability. For it is by its place, size, energy, and growth by material composition —qualities all involving external and variable relations —that a geometrical body existing differs from a geometrical solid defined. Aristotle himself derived the existence of any particular thing or substance not from its metaphysical components but from prior complete natural beings; and he even assigned to this ancestral matter what seems to us too fixed a form, since he did not admit any evolution of species. Even if by chance he had been right in respect to the natural history of earthly animals, the same matter in other cycles or in other worlds might evidently have displayed a different morphology. The matter which by taking a particular form becomes a particular thing need never have worn that form before and may never wear it again. Its career is open towards the infinite. Though at each moment it must be something specific, yet, if we consider its unknown plastic stress and the incalculable accidents to which it may be subject, we shall hardly be able to hold it down to any other enduring characters than those involved in its distinctive function: which is to lend existence to certain essences in a certain order, and enable them to succeed and to confront one another in a competitive world.

How penetrate into the inner flow of this existence? Sensuous, dialectical, or moral views of it, however legiti-

This flux not to be understood in graphic terms.

mate, are necessarily summary, superficial, and poetical, being created by a psyche biassed and synthetic in her reactions. Mathematical views are more impartial, but wretchedly abstract. Thus, for instance, number is a just category to apply to the field of action, since its elements move as units, but it is a miserable essence to substitute for them. Accurate science has this defect, that it seems to describe the distribution of units of nothing, and to record averages in movements that elude sense, and yet are conceived and posited only in reference to pictorial objects. Meantime existence is no spectacle, though spectacles and calculations may amuse or describe it. In ourselves, and in the objects on our own plane encountered in action, existence is a strain and an incubus, particular, self-centred, substantial. It is in terms of such existence, unstable but burdened and concrete, that an unsophisticated natural philosophy might conceive the realm of matter.

If there is to be lapse, the flux at each point must possess an essence from which it lapses. These points,

Idea of a natural moment.

which are the terms of any possible change, I will call *natural moments*. By natural moments, I do not mean instants or cross-sections of the whole flux, where everything is supposed simultaneous; I mean rather any concrete but ultimate elements in the web of existence, within which there is no change or variation of essence, yet which are not merely their essences, but events exemplifying those essences, facts generated and dated in a general flux that outruns them on every side.   Within each natural moment there can be no temporal divisions or scale; if a duration is assigned to it at all distinguishable from its intrinsic being, it must be assigned by virtue of some external measure or scale, drawn from an alien medium or perspective in which the moment is supposed to be embedded.   In its own person, a natural moment may be called lasting or instantaneous with equal propriety; for its quality is unchangeable, and any variation would simply divide it into several natural moments; it contains no temporal diversity by which it could be collated with different points in a dated scale of time.   On the other hand, this undivided moment has material continuity with other moments which generate it and which it generates, so that its life is but one incident, an indivisible beat between states of existence which are not itself yet are its closest kin.

In what does this kinship consist?   Not merely in similarity, though some similarity—perhaps only quantitative—is doubtless involved in derivation. Its
A natural moment may be followed by a cata- transitive
strophe and by chaos.   Nor is derivation mere essence.
juxtaposition, since we have seen that there is no prior medium in which this juxtaposition could occur. There must, then, be something in the inner nature of one natural moment that renders it the derivative from another natural moment, therefore called its source, and productive of a third natural moment which we therefore call its effect.   Every natural moment is both traditional and propulsive.   It has a beginning and an end, a head and a tail—the head turned towards the end, and the tail towards the beginning.   These need not be distinct members within its body; they may be distinguished, like up and down, only by virtue of contrary contacts and tensions; for a natural moment bears quite

opposite relations to its source and food on the one side, and to its effects or relics on the other. Many rays, as it were, are focussed in each explosion; and the spark dies by diffusion or excretion of the substance which lent it spasmodic being. Its essence is like that of a valve: it contains a reference to the direction in which matter may flow through it. The moment exists only in act, when the valve is a valve in function; and at that crisis it yields to pressure coming from one side only, while it opens out and empties itself only towards the other side. Or we might liken it to a hyphen or to the sign + ; essentially transitional, as it is existentially transitory. By essence, it overlooks its neighbours on either hand without trespassing on their ground. That a thing by its internal being should have reference to something external—a fact which in the case of knowledge gives so much trouble to logicians—is so far from being an anomaly or an exception that it is the indispensable condition of existing at all: because, apart from that transcendent tension or inherent instability, a natural moment would be simply its essence, and not the act of reaching and dropping that essence, as it must be if it exists or takes place in nature.

I do not think that analytically transition can be otherwise expressed than as a transformation of one

Transition though unintelligible, may be symbolised dramatically or scientifically: it comports a forward tension within the moment.

thing into another, involving two natural moments, and leaving the bond between them obscure. But it is not analytically that transition may be understood; it is lost when its terms are divided; and yet it is no synthesis of these terms, but a generation—whatever that may be—of one term out of the other. Within each term, however, we may expect to find a synthetic symbol and counterpart of transition. Let me call it the *forward tension* of the natural moment. This name is not meant to attribute to the elements of the flux any conscious effort or expectancy; they are restless without the feeling of unrest; yet the analogy implied in the metaphor must be a real analogy, since effort and expectancy are creatures and expressions of this very tension in the flux of matter, when it takes the form of a psyche. *Forward tension*, then, will designate fairly enough whatsoever corresponds, within a natural moment, to the external fact that it occurs between two others, one of which an observer would call its antecedent and the other its consequent. Such a synthetic burden, native to existence in its every node or concretion, may well be represented in physics by a quantum of potential energy, determined by some formula or equation; and we know that the ignorant psyche creates many a poetic index to this same burden in herself, when she conceives sentimental time, and all the dramatic perspectives that people the imagination; for it is only by virtue of the tensions concentrated within her own organism—her memory, will, and intelligence—that the psyche is able to paint a world, which she thinks real, on the canvas of intuition.

That the natural moment has a forward tension becomes the more plausible, or even certain, when we consider that we are describing elements of existence (not mathematical or dialectical patterns, which analysis might discover there) and that the field of existence is simply the field of action: for there is no doubt that in action a forward tension is inherent. Nor is it the agent only that has this movement; we have found that his partner in action, the brotherworld on which he acts, must have it too, if they are to play the same game, and contribute to the same sequel. We may therefore confidently attribute the forward tension proper to our life to all the rest of nature, down to its primary elements, without attributing to those elements, or to that total,

The nature of natural moments may be found written large in the conventional or dramatic moments of human experience.

any specifically human quality. On the contrary, that forward tension in us is precisely what we share with all matter, and what renders matter our great companion; for the realms of essence and of truth, to which the spirit looks when it suspends action, are not so much our companions or enemies in this world as our celestial monitors: their perpetual presence does not beset us here but, if we notice it, transports us there. We may therefore appeal to our experience of action on the human scale to suggest to us the nature of action even in the heart of matter, which a mere diminution of mathematical scale or use of the microscope may never reach.

Now, on the human scale, the most obvious units in action are men, and their forward tension is dramatically called their will. A man's body, if we study it analytically, is enormously complex, and his will highly conditioned and insecure, so that he thinks it free; but if we take him and his will in the flush of action, as factors in the moral world, they count as units. Each personage in history, each passion or interest in a man's life, may be called a conventional moment. Considered dramatically, each is a single phase of existence internally constant, through which existence is precipitated into its next phase. How these conventional moments begin, how they end, how matter flows through them, and what determines their inner character while they last are all matters of common knowledge: we call them birth, death, food, and influence. It is on this analogy that natural moments should be conceived, if we wish to avoid the extravagances of pure theory usurping the place of fact.

A man, with the forward tension of all his instincts
Birth and and passions, notoriously springs from a seed;
death are and he develops from the heart of that seed,
proper to
all natural internally, as it transforms and organises the
moments. food which comes to it and which it selects.
Seed and food: these are the conditions *a parte priori*

of a man's existence; a seed, to transmit the centre of organisation and impose its specific hereditary form; and food to supply suitable matter to pass through that form and sustain it in existence. So this conventional moment, this individual life, begins and is established: and how does it end? By dissolution, when that hereditary formative energy is exhausted, or crushed by accident, and the matter which it had organised about its centre is dispersed. This matter will take other forms, some of them living; it may breed worms, as the Christian imagination was fond of repeating; but a corpse is not a seed; it is not from there that the next generation is derived; their seed must be plucked from the secret heart of the man in his maturity, essentially uncontrolled and uncontaminated by his personal fortunes. There is a vast difference in character between the beginning and the end: the source is single, concentrated, specific, loaded with precise potentialities; the effects and consequences are diffused, peripheral, miscellaneous, unending. Except the seed of his children, all that a man sheds during his life and at his death is, from the vital point of view, corruption; all that he draws in, in so far as it feeds his flame, is purity and life. He is a pulsation or diastole of his hereditary nature, a bubble waxing till it bursts.

Existence, then, is a passage from potentiality to act, the order of its moments being determined by the direction of realisation within each of them. Before and after are not relations in a pure time, but organic, like up and down or right and left. They presuppose a centre, a focus into which matter flows and from which it is dispersed; and this concretion, like a spark or a blow, is irreversible, and separates its occasion and materials on the one hand, in which it was potential, from its effects and remains on

Actualisation has a direction even within the moment, due to the matter passing through that form.

the other, in which its potentiality is that of other things. Thus existence is not simply a series of essences solidified, nor a juxtaposition of phenomena; it is the career of a hereditary substance, it is the Life of Matter. And this in both senses of the word life: for it is the history of the fortunes of that plastic enduring being, and it is also the forward tension intrinsic to each moment of that career: an inner tension which is sometimes raised to consciousness and turns to spiritual light, but which animates matter everywhere and renders it transitional. Matter, as if ashamed at the irrationality of having one form rather than another, hastens to exchange it, whatever it may be, for some other form, and this haste is its whole reality; for it can add nothing to the essences which it successively exemplifies except just this: that they are enabled to be exemplified in succession, to be picked up and abandoned. Matter is the invisible wind which, sweeping for no reason over the field of essences, raises some of them into a cloud of dust: and that whirlwind we call existence.

Potentiality seems a vain word, and deceptive; yet it indicates a fact in the realm of truth, since seeds are

Potentiality a retrospective name for material fertility.
capable of development into certain organisms only, and these cannot spring from any other source. Yet what this potentiality may be actually is usually unknown to us; we merely assume that it must be something actual, since the state of the seed at any one time must exemplify some individual essence, however complex it may be. Not that this actual state of the potential would pass into the further state, potential in it, if the potential were merely an essence, or a pure phenomenon; an essence or pure phenomenon has no fertility, no implications; it will remain for ever just what it is. It is matter, impatient of form, that fills form with a forward tension, and realises one essence after another; and this tension in matter is ultimately expressed and

rendered conscious in spirit; so that spirit is normally filled with craving, fear, curiosity, and jealousy, clasping to its bosom something precious and unintelligible, only too apt to slip away.

The relation between a man and his father and that between his son and himself, considered in its essence, is identical in the two instances, and always bilateral: there cannot be a child without a parent nor a parent without a child. Yet the flux runs only one way, and from the point of view of each person the felt tensions in the two instances are unilateral, different, and opposite. Even if by miracle grandfather and grandson were identical in essence—as in Greece they often bore the same name— they would be separated and posited as distinct persons by their opposite unilateral relation to the man between, who was son only to the one, and father only to the other. By these contrasting offices and sentiments each generation synthesises the flux of life in its own feeling and action at every moment; and we may reasonably regard this double tension as representing, on the human scale, the irreversible polarity within every natural moment, which indicates and transmits the irreversible direction of genesis.

Nor is this universal flux composed of a single strand, like a thin autobiographical melody, sounding only one note at a time. It is many-voiced, like the sea of Homer. We may indeed divide it ideally into instants, each of which cuts through the whole stream and shows its complex visceral face at that juncture; but such a cross-section is not a natural moment. A natural moment is a realised essence of any sort, so long as its realisation continues; and there may be many collateral natural moments. Moments will be collateral if, when traced backwards or forwards according to their inward tensions, they terminate in identical ulterior moments;

Instances of parent and child.

Lateral tensions involved.

and this without being strictly simultaneous through-out the interval, nor divisible on the same scale. So streams that flow from the same lake and empty into the same estuary need not be identical or equal or parallel but must be collateral. Scientific speculation now seems to authorise this view, even for the purposes of calculation, which I should not have expected; but a sceptic will readily admit that the more the sciences deepen their view and discount their assumptions the more they will familiarise us with differences of pace in nature, and incommensurable meanderings. Yet not meanderings beyond the field of action, into a metaphysical region: for unless all these scales and dimensions impinge upon facts posited and acted upon by animal faith, their interesting variety will belong only to the realm of essence, and will not describe this world. This world is not easily probed or understood. Existence is nothing if not complex, elastic, funda-mentally chaotic. Perception, description, and dogma over-simplify and over-regulate everything.

All lateral tensions might be typified, for a living being, in the horrid simultaneity of eating and being eaten. Microbes devour no less efficaciously than wild beasts; and this perpetual inner waste, met by the need of replenishment, is the clearest of demonstrations that matter is the principle of existence. Matter is essentially *food*, an object of competition and a substance fit for assimilation. It is for ever withdrawing itself from one form and assuming another, or being redigested. Food is substance in circulation, shuffling its unities like figures in a dance; and the same generative transition that originally establishes a particular moment of existence is required to maintain and renew it; otherwise that essence is lost. Every living thing must feed, feed perpetually, or it dissolves.

Living beings must be fed laterally if they are to persist recognis-ably.

If, then, we may transfer these fundamental characters of conventional moments to natural moments, we may say that a natural noment arises and exists only by virtue of external supports; first a parent moment to launch it and determine its initial character, and then collateral moments to control that heritage and determine what, and how long, it shall be in act. If ever existence is sustained at all in what we call the same object, or person, or thought, this happens by an external equilibrium which keeps that thing in a state of suspense or of continual self-recovery: each of its external relations tending to transform it, yet all of them together, for the nonce, keeping it as it was.

Lateral tensions condition the formation and exertion of forward tension in any particular moment.

A seed, if it could be thoroughly inspected by a clairvoyant spirit, would reveal the essence which contains or prepares its pregnancy, according to the method of development prevalent in nature, or in that species. But the actual essence of the seed, or of its ultimate fruit, is nothing to the naturalist; for he knows that no seed will mature except under certain fostering external conditions; and to these conditions, not to the unknown essence of the seed, he will trace and attribute the issue. The seed itself could never have been formed or, as it were, expelled from the parent moment, without the food and warmth of a fostering world; and in the act of birth or existence—for these are one in a natural moment—the sequel will be determined and sustained by the lateral tensions which beset it, allowing that sequel and forbidding any other. Everything, then, seems to be a mechanism of circumstances, of which the essences realised at distinct moments are, for the naturalist, only idle signs.

What seems to follow? That the forward tension which I have been attributing to natural moments may be simply the act of escaping in the direction of least

H

resistance, as matter always will. The mysterious
potentiality packed in the seed would then not be
internal to it, or due to a specially wonderful
essence therein embodied. It would be the
concentration there of many external relations
at work together, a resultant of all the cosmic
tensions to which that point was subject. In itself
the seed or the moment would not then need to possess
any specific character: it might have only a simple
or neutral essence, such perhaps as the pure Being
which filled the atoms of Democritus; yet, without
manifesting any particular bias, it might be ready, as
far as its quantity availed, to run and nourish any
vortex then evolving, or any self-asserting form. This
it would do or not do, according to circumstances;
so that all the tensions and heritages of animal life
would be but incidents in a universal mechanism.

They may form a universal mechanism.

A diviner like Democritus, or like a modern mathematician hypostatising his notation into the substance
of the world, may be willing to prophesy that
such is the actual constitution of the universe.
Such it may be indeed, at some inhuman
depth; and I am willing to admit any such
hypothesis on the authority of the learned,
because that seems to me to be the direction in
which the truth must lie, even if I distrust the
means by which those wise men think they have discovered it. Yet however perfectly such a system might
transcribe the flux of existence, it would not *be* that
flux in person, or in its lapsing life; and science cannot
well be truer of it, though true at a deeper level, than
are all the vulgar essences which visibly give it character.
Somehow the flux has actually gathered and distilled
itself into many-coloured natural moments, as into
drops; and these are the first and fundamental measures
by which we may measure it, and the centres from
which we must survey it.

The doctrine that all matter is similar and all laws constant is a mere speculation.

Perhaps in a chaos the only forward tension might be that of the universe as a whole, distended and convulsed by all its lateral tensions indiscriminately. Chaos, however, though doubtless fundamental, is not now complete. If it were, it would not be observable for lack of observers; and we, so long as we behold a world, however chaotic, have the assurance that the flux, for the time being, has been somewhat canalised in our parts of the universe, and that lateral tensions are partly held in check, and turned to sustenance, for the benefit of some persisting organisms; and the forward tensions of these, with their variations and fulfilments, form the drama of natural history.

Moreover, if we may say that in the world at large lateral tensions determine the existence and the forward tension of every part, we may also say, *vice versa*, that the forward tensions of the parts, taken together and meeting, compose the lateral tensions at work at that time; and this way of speaking has some advantages. It recognises that material existence, though everywhere conditioned externally, is everywhere spontaneous. Neither its being nor its singular forward tension are in the least questionable or unwelcome to any innocent moment. It takes itself for granted and leaps, if it can, to the full expansion of its inner powers. That act, or that attempt, is its very existence. Once existing, the moment unhesitatingly exercises its native force in its innate direction, and acts no less freely and efficaciously than it is acted upon. In a contingent world necessity is a conspiracy of accidents.

In any case the flux is spontaneous in the part no less than in the whole.

This precipitation of accidents is the work of matter, shifting its equilibrium and modifying its strains. A flux could neither change nor continue if it were immaterial. Its successive forms, since it takes them up and drops them, are not essences without substance nor facts without

It is inseparable from matter.

derivation. A natural moment marks the existential emergence of a new form—that particular form which circumstances then impose on the matter at hand, as previously disposed; and this moment ends when the balance of tensions which brought it about yields to a fresh equilibrium. This limit of any moment is and is called an end, as that other limit is and is called a beginning; for here there is concretion and there release. The forms are eternal, the matter is old; yet the interplay of the two is full of novelty, and at each point takes a somewhat unprecedented direction. For it is not the old form that creates the new; the old form, if it could do anything, would simply preserve itself; but it is indomitable matter, from the beginning in unstable equilibrium, that fell once into that old form as it falls now into the new, spontaneously and without vows of fidelity. Its potentiality, though unborn, is always specific, since it is involved in the distribution and tensions of the actual matter already in play; its realisation is the flux of existence, creating succession and telling the beads of time.

The dominance of matter in every existing being, even when that being is spiritual, is the great axiom of materialism, to which this whole book is only a corollary. But this axiom would not be consonant with the life of nature if it did not involve a complementary truth which takes away all its partisan bias and half its inhuman sting: I mean the complementary truth that matter is no model devised by the human imagination, like Egyptian atoms or the laws of physics, but is a primeval plastic substance of unknown potentiality, perpetually taking on new forms; the gist of materialism being that these forms are all passive and precarious, while the plastic stress of matter is alone creative and, as far as we can surmise, indestructible.

CHAPTER VI

TROPES

EVENTS have a form as much as things have: even the Greeks, those lovers of statues, were far from insensible to the essence of tragedy or of a happy life. Notion of Now the form of an event is not that event a trope. itself. An event, as I take the word, means a portion of the flux of existence; it is a conventional moment, like the birth of Christ or the battle of Waterloo, composed of natural moments generating one another in a certain order, and embedded in a particular context of other events: so that each event is a particular and can occur only once. Only the *type* of such a sequence, composed of such moments, is the *form* of the event, and this form is a universal. It need never have occurred; if I had said the resurrection of Christ, instead of his birth, the reader might have his doubts about it. The fact that such an essence was exemplified somewhere in an event would be a historical truth; in order to substantiate it, the flux of matter must assume that form; without this material and incidental illustration that type of sequence would remain in the air, in the realm of fiction or of theory. It is especially important at this point to dispel that confusion between essences and facts which makes a quicksand of all philosophy. I will therefore give a separate name to the essence of any event, as

101

distinguished from that event itself, and call it a
trope.

In what precisely does an event differ from the
trope which it exemplifies? I reply (for I must be
A trope
is not an
event. brief): in being enacted. Any substance differs
from the essence of that substance, and any
event from the essence of that event, in that
it can arise and perish, and this in two ways: externally,
by intruding into a field of irrelevant entities, or quitting that field; and then again internally, by changing
the order of its parts, each of which, in a thing or an
event, has an individuality internal to it, and is a concrete component, not merely a fragment or aspect of
the whole. Things and events are contingent and they
are compound, even if monotonous or continuously
similar: whereas their essences are eternal, and even
when complex are not compound but absolutely in-
dissoluble.

Now, in a flux, the total essence realised in the form
of its flow during any particular period obviously
cannot be realised in any one of its moments, when
only this moment exists: it can be realised only
progressively, by the order in which those moments
arise and vanish. This order is the trope; it is the
essence of that sequence seen under the form of
eternity; and since existence, in this event, has realised
that essence, that essence has descriptive value in
respect to this world. It belongs to the realm of
truth.

For this reason, a trope is not on the same plane
of being as a perspective, because it is not relative to
A trope
not a per-
spective. any point of view or native to any psyche: a
perspective is only specious, whilst a trope is
formal. The flux, of its own initiative and
in its own person, falls into that order composed of
those elements, whether anyone observes it or not;
the trope is a historical truth, the perspective is a

historical impression. But these relative impressions or perspectives could never arise if substance and the flux of substance had no essence of their own to begin with: that would be tantamount to saying that substance was nothing, that there were no moments and no centres, and that there was no difference between a flux and what was not a flux. The nature of existence is to possess whatsoever nature it possesses with a treacherous emphasis, dragging that essence, by a sort of rape, from its essential context into contingent relations; those relations, being contingent, are variable; and the flux is merely the realisation of this intrinsic variability involved in existence. The flux is accordingly always tracing some path through the realm of essence, and at every point assumes an assignable posture: that is to say, while each natural moment enriches the flux with its intrinsic quality, the existence of that moment comes by a transformation of the substance which flows through it and unites it in a determinate trope with its antecedents and its consequents.

Thus, in order to describe an event we need to look forward and back along the path of change, and to note what each included moment which we are It describes able to distinguish had for its origin and for its some results. Observation then discovers a trope, embedded but unless this trope spans all existence, and in existence. extends endlessly or to some absolute end of time, the total event which it defines will be like the natural moments composing it, a mere episode; and this episode, observed because we happen to belong to the same epoch, will be caught on the wing, leaving a margin before, behind, and around it of unexplored contingency. The embosoming reality, by virtue of which this whole episode takes its place in nature, will remain unknown. The mind cannot pursue the roots of things into the darkness; it cannot discover why they exist;

it must be satisfied with noting their passing aspect, which is but an essence; and it must follow the chase, carried by its own galloping substance, to see what aspect they may wear next. The flux, or the path of existence, will elude us if we are content to express it lyrically, by eliciting the intrinsic essences of its single moments; but it may be partly described dramatically, in epic tropes, in terms which are formulæ or types of sequence.

Tropes are not necessarily exhaustive even of that part of the flux in which they may be discovered: *Tropes are of many sorts, interwoven and superposed.* many heterogeneous tropes may run on together, or may appear once only, like a lost thought. When a man is speaking, there are tropes in his language; every word uttered being a trope, as well as all inflections and forms of syntax. But these cannot live detached, in a realm of grammar; they can live only when grafted on the wholly different tropes of the nervous system, heart-beats, and circulation of the blood; and these biological tropes are again embedded in others of longer span, belonging to natural and political history. All these measures are more or less on the human scale, familiar but treacherous; because they in turn can only live if supported and filled out by minute incessant vibrations, molecular and ethereal, or by whatever else may mark the primary pulse of nature. In this complex of changes, perhaps endless tropes might be distinguished by a tireless and ingenious observer. Each animal and each philosopher picks out those which fall in with the rhythms and oppositions of his own habits and thoughts: a mile means a thousand paces, and we measure all things by our own stride. These measures are not false on that account; on the contrary, they are true, since the tropes of human existence are natural tropes, belonging to the same flux as all the others, and capable of being their measure. But they are not exclusive, nor exhaustive, nor pre-eminent: and superstition consists in thinking them so.

A sceptic, fearing to fall into such superstition, might even complain that all tropes were merely impressionistic units; that, in fact, they were nothing but perspectives, and that in supposing them to be more, I and all other men (including himself when not sceptical) were dupes of our human interests and habits. But the oversight and self-contradiction inherent in scepticism recurs here unabashed. In obeying our habits and interests we are masters, not dupes; our habits and interests are themselves tropes that must have been established victoriously in the flux, if living creatures defined by those tropes are able to lift their heads out of it and to survey it, no matter how relatively and how partially. Everything cannot be merely imputed. Imputation itself must exist actively, in centres and on occasions which are not imputed but actual. If for instance space, time, and matter were not characterised by definite properties and modes of being, separating them from non-entity and distinguishing them from one another, they would be simply nothing. If in the region indicated by these names— for we use them indicatively in perception and by animal faith—there is anything at all, it must possess the essence which it possesses, of which these names are partial suggestions; although, of course, the true essence of that substance need not at all resemble the images which, in using those names, may occupy any man's fancy.

Scepticism, then, need not be turned into a dogma, into absolute relativism, solipsism, or idealism, nor into a denial of substance and of truth. On the contrary, a scepticism sceptical of itself may become a method of discovery, and in challenging superficial tropes it may reveal deeper ones. And here, in the words " interest " and " habit " I think we have a hint of a principle

applicable to the criticism of tropes. No trope is exclusive, as if it could prevent the parallel, higher, lower,
or intertwined development of other tropes;
The most
repeated but some tropes are *repeated*; they are habitual
are the most
ingrained. modes of action or measures constantly maintained; and this circumstance distinguishes
them from local harmonies, often the most important
æsthetically, which arise only once, by an unprecedented
union of circumstances. The advent of Christianity, of
the Renaissance, and of the Reformation are important
tropes never, we may presume, to be repeated; but
birth and death are perpetual in nature, and the habits
and passions of each creature, while it lives, are principles of reiteration; they involve repetitions in action,
and they find and use repetitions in nature, answering to
their own precision of form. Organisms are instruments
of repetition; and they rely, for their existence and
prosperity, on the repetition of opportunities for the
repetition of their acts. Were this reliance not justified, or this mechanism unstable, there could be
no life, experience, or art in the world. The more
exactly and the more pervasively a trope repeats itself
the more it introduces us, if we discover it, into the
heart of the flux, and the better it supplies us with
an instrument and a background for tracing such
rarer tropes as may be discernible occasionally, or
such as may arise only once. Moreover, repetition
of itself marks the beginning and the end of a trope
and rescues it from the arbitrary scope of human
apperception.

Tropes realised only once—like the whole history
of the world, if there be such a total—are resultant
Only a
pervasive
trope can
be funda-
mental. harmonies, which only emotion could regard
as reasons for their own existence. Tropes
realised occasionally leave open the question
of their incidence: why do they appear at
certain junctures and not at others? If no reason can

be given, the flux to that extent is found to be chaotic.
If on the contrary their initiation is regular, they are
parts of a universal trope, which requires them at
those junctures, and connects their occasions by a
mechanism deeper than they. This universal trope will
be realised everywhere, and contained, not interrupted,
in the realisation of all supervening occasional tropes.
The flux can be truly and surely measured only by
tropes which repeat themselves uninterruptedly on
their own plane.

Such a trope is called mechanical: so that to say
that the world is fundamentally mechanical is the
evident alternative to saying that it is funda- Mechanism
mentally chaotic. Nor is it merely by a play is the
on words, or a sort of divination, that we are alternative
to chaos.
justified in saying so: the thing follows from
our original trust in the possibility of action, which is
the criterion of existence, and the test of substantiality.
The agent and his world must both be compacted of
matter moving in constant and recurring tropes, if the
one is not to be mad and the other treacherous. Men
of the world, and women even with more assurance,
are quick to foresee or to divine what *must* be going on.
Naturally they express this insight in loose human
terms; but the trust in repetition and in mechanism is
there, else all penetration and all policy would be pre-
cluded. To turn this imaginative insight into science
is merely a matter of attentive observation, measurement,
and transcription of current metaphors into technical
terms. The behaviour of animals would then appear
to be scanned by tropes continuous with those which
scan the behaviour of matter everywhere, if not identical with them. Madness and wild originality, like
volcanoes and tornadoes, will be of the greatest help
in hastening this assimilation; because the level of
mechanism is so deep and its scale so far from the
human that it is better revealed in cataclysms, miracles,

and diseases than in the placid course of superficial experience.

All this, however, is said in general and from a transcendental point of view: it prejudges nothing as to the particular mechanism which may actually be fundamental. In any case, in calling tropes mechanical, because by hypothesis constantly repeated, we must not assume that they are mathematically necessary, or not vital, or simple, or exclusive. On the contrary, they are contingent and arbitrary, since they are forms of existence, which might just as easily have possessed any other character. They are spanned by all sorts of other tropes, including those native to the human senses and to human logic. They are radically " vital ", if this word means spontaneous and irreducible to any alien principle. As to their simplicity, that is perhaps only a relation to human alacrity or bewilderment in their presence, and no property of their substance or essence. Forms of flux can never be quite simple, since they must contain several terms; in existence they are hardly separable from the tensions which realise them, which probably extend to infinity; so that to speak of simplicity is rather a sign of it in us, than a serious postulate of science.

The fundamental trope arbitrary, vital, not exclusive, and hardly simple.

There is a reason why comparatively simple tropes, called laws, are discoverable in those parts of nature, like the heavens, which we observe from a great distance, and also in those parts, like the depths of matter, which we cannot observe at all, but may imagine in terms relative to their gross aspects and motions. Distance and theory act like a sieve: they eliminate all the detail and leave only average results or total impressions, conveyed by special and highly selective media, such as light and mathematical calculation. The *picture* thus pro-

Laws: how discerned and in what sense true.

duced, if there be a picture at all, is a pure fiction, a
visual or phonetic symbol perfectly subjective and
human; but the law enunciated may be true; that is,
the flux may actually pass through the series of abstract
positions selected, and in its moving equilibrium may
satisfy the equations expressed in the law.

When tropes are called laws, there is danger of
idolatry: for although scientific philosophers often
warn us that a law is merely a formula or an
average, or an equation probably approxi- Law as a
mately realised in a certain plane of events, physical
yet this probability lets loose our action and idol.
expectation; and the force of expectation projects its
confidence into a myth; it erects Law into a metaphysical power compelling events to obey it. This
is the great idol, I will not say of science, but of the
passions which science subserves. Images are as
indispensable in science as they are in worship; a
thorough iconoclast, who should banish all images,
poetical and mathematical no less than sensuous, would
simply make a desert of the mind, and destroy all
science, like all religion; but these necessary images
are vehicles, not ultimate objects of regard. The
quick mind passes through them, here to the instant
fact, there to the supreme essence.

I think that the reality of law can be briefly expressed in two maxims: one, that whatsoever happens
anywhere, happens there spontaneously, as Natural
if it had never occurred before and would causation
never occur again; the other, that whatso- spontane-
ever spontaneously happens once will have habitual.
spontaneously happened before and will spontaneously happen again, wherever similar elements are in
the same relations. The first of these maxims proclaims the contingency, substantiality, originality of
fact everywhere: it is the axiom of empiricism, when
experience is understood practically and not psycho-

logically. The second maxim proclaims the postulate of action and of reason called the uniformity of nature. It is only a postulate, which contingent, substantial, and original facts may at any point disallow; but in so far as they do so, they revert to chaos and render life and art difficult, if not impossible.

" The reign of law " is accordingly only a modern and bombastic equivalent for the ancient naturalness of nature. In so far as the law is more rigid than a habit, it is a human artifice of notation. In so far as it indicates a co-operative march of events mutually generated and destroyed, it is another name for the ways of nature or of God, for the forms which existence can show to spirit. But nature, though highly favourable to spirit, since she has bred it, is not governed by her child; and even in our familiar world the wide margin of incalculable properties by which the calculable part of nature is surrounded—what we sometimes call her secondary and tertiary qualities—proves this most curiously; for in the world of action, as spirit conceives it, spirit itself seems superfluous. And perhaps even in that calculable skeleton of primary qualities, selected because they can be measured and predicted in mathematical tropes, there may be a margin of error; for a law is an essence, eternally identical, and nature is in flux, and probably never the same. Very likely all the movements of matter are more or less elastic or organic: I mean responsive afresh to a total environment never exactly repeated, so that no single law would perfectly define all consecutive changes even in the plane of matter, and every response would be that of a new-born organism to an unprecedented world. There would be nothing magical in this: it would merely distribute the radical contingency of existence throughout its successive phases, without concentrating it in a single initial fact and initial law. But on the human scale, and for

fashioning perishable human works, such fundamental
instability in nature would remain negligible. Even
in a land of earthquakes we live in houses.

Belief in law when hasty is called superstition or,
when more cautious, empiricism: but the principle in
both cases is the same. Both take expecta- The hazard
tion for probability; and what probability in empiri-
can there be that an expectation, arising at in super-
one point, should define a law for the whole stition.
universe? Expectation is an animal attitude resting
not at all on induction or probability, but on the fact
that animals are wound up to do certain things and
vaguely but confidently posit a world in which their
readiness may become action. In superstition, as in
empiricism, we yield to the vital temptation to ignore
reason, and we trust to courage and to whatever idea
is uppermost in the mind. Yet in a roundabout way,
on the scale and in the period of that animal life, this
blind courage is normally justified by the event. For
how should the psyche be ready and eager for a particular employment, if in her long evolution she had
not been moulded to just that employment by a world
which allowed and rewarded it? How should potentialities and propensities be more deeply rooted in her
than in the world of which she is an integral part?
Certainly, her ideas are specious and her passions
precipitate; yet for all their delusions and disarray,
they have brought her forward, and she survives; so
that things expected, hoped for, and worked for by
any prospering animal, are, on the whole and with a
difference, likely to happen.

There is then no necessity in the relation between
cause and effect, and no assurance that law is Natural
constant. Nevertheless, causation is prevalent: status of
were it not prevalent in fact, the expecta- tropes
tion of it could never have arisen. But the and laws.
validity of a prevalent law lies simply in its function as

a measure of events; it is no adequate description of them, much less a power bringing them about. Obviously the complete and actual march of events cannot be reduced to anything else than its full and precise self: and even its complete form, being an essence, would be, if considered apart, in another realm from its manifestation. There is no constraint to exist native to these tropes, but it may be true that the flux, which must exhibit some form or other, does for a time and in a certain dimension exhibit this particular trope, or, as we say, obeys this law. A mathematical or pictorial skeleton is thus traced by the economy of thought within the body of nature, leaving all the other dimensions and all the other tropes to hang like garlands about those calculated supports. The skeleton exists, in the sense that by hypothesis this law prevails now in this region; but it is no skeleton in its operative function, like that of an animal; it is no rigid substance within the soft substance of events; it is only a trope, which the thrifty mind selects from the tangle of relations which hold those facts in the mesh of existence. The selection is not made arbitrarily, but in sympathy with the scale and character of the action which that thrifty mind follows in its fortunes and prophesies in its thoughts.

Many a divergence among philosophers may be understood and dispelled by this consideration: that the fundamental tropes in nature, far from excluding other tropes, inevitably produce them. When things are in motion, new relations arise among them by a necessary magic, and they lend themselves to description in various

Necessary inadequacy of tropes to describe the full reality.

logics or anatomies without interrupting their habitual flux. It is never a just objection to the reality of any trope that it may not be the exclusive trope in the movement of existence, or that there are events which it cannot properly measure. Mathematical tropes may

pervade the realm of matter, supporting occasional
moral and æsthetic tropes which supervene on the
mathematical tropes without interrupting them.

Tropes, mathematical or vital, mechanical or historical, all belong to the region of Platonic Ideas; they
are unitary patterns distinguishable in the
movement of things; they are no part of the
moving substance executing those patterns
and overflowing them. Yet, if any mind is
to perceive that flux, or to distinguish any of
its phases, it cannot do so otherwise than by
discerning some essence exemplified there, which limits
one phase or one moment and divides it from another.
Of itself existence has no wholeness: it would not be
existence if it were not scattered into moments, each
its own centre, reaching out towards one another in
the dark, forgetting what they were in what they
become, and learning what they will be only by
becoming it. It is the very function of flux and of
volume in the flux, it is the singular virtue of physical
time and space, to make it possible that incompatible
things should be equally actual, and irrelevant things
closely conjoined. For when anything is actual, the
existence of any ulterior thing becomes, to that living
moment, eventual, and unnecessary: whether that
ulterior thing arises or fails to arise, whether somewhere else it once existed or did not exist, makes no
difference here. No difference, I mean, in the instant
fact: for that by subterranean processes or substantial
derivation, this moment has followed upon others, and
will issue in others again, is, if true, an additional
circumstance, curious but, in principle, subsidiary: for
each of those other moments, and every physical bond
between them, would still have to realise and posit
itself on its own account, as this moment posits and
realises itself here. The brute fact might be enlarged,
but it would necessarily remain insulated and absolute

Being essences, they diversify, but cannot control, existence.

I

in its contingency. No moment, no event, and no world can insure the existence or the character of anything beyond it.

How, then, impose on all existence some trope exhibited by it here and now, and trust that trope to be universal? Why should the flux submit to reproducing this particular pattern, instead of bringing others to light? The contingency of existence is pervasive, and the stress of it may be everywhere much the same, but the forms of existence are likely to be always, as we recede from any fact, increasingly different. The repetitions are as contingent as the novelties; each field of repetition, if we extend the range of observation beyond its limits, proves itself a novelty, as does every species of animal, every art, and every idea. Even if, in fact, some trope is perpetually recurrent, or if one little unchanging world is suspended for ever in the midst of a vacuum destined never to be peopled by other worlds, still this final truth is an accident and almost a paradox: for why should this universe have come to be so trim, when the infinity of essence was tempting it to be otherwise?

It follows that whenever a trope of any sort has been distinguished and found to prevail in nature, as far as our knowledge extends, it need by no means prevail beyond the limit of this domesticated region, nor above or below the level of our human sensibility. It need not even exclude anomalies and outbreaks of chaos in the interstices of the prevalent tropes. In viewing any part of nature as a unit, as we do in the act of discovering a trope, we have necessarily substituted an essence for it. For this reason essences only can be data: the fact which has aroused this intuition and which we posit in these sensuous or grammatical terms, necessarily transcends these terms, and every ideal synthesis of them. It exists on its own moving plane, by tension towards

Their prevalence is conditional.

ulterior facts and by relation to them. Our intuition is a snapshot: the image it creates yields a word, a law, a *logos* in another realm of being from the flux which confronts it. The tropes which we call the laws of nature cannot therefore exclude other and contrary manifestations of what nature secretly contains. Egotism and credulity may protect most of us from troubling about those foreign possibilities; if there comes any startling failure in our presumptions—any miracle or paradox—we are inclined to believe that the marvel responds to our private interests even more directly and surely than does the familiar routine of the world; and the more remote and eccentric the comet that intrudes into our skies, the clearer proof we read in it of our home faith. Everything is indeed a support for the religious spirit, when that spirit is addressed to the truth; but when it is addressed to imposing on the universe its own animal habits and animal prosperity, the farther it ranges the more it is likely to find itself out in the cold.

For fear of this unhomeliness of the infinite, some philosophers in all ages have adopted a heroic way of asserting the absolute domination of their acquired science: they have supposed that the history of the world is self-repeating and comes round for ever in a circle. Infinity and familiarity are thus reconciled; and the limited evidences of human knowledge do not prevent it from claiming unlimited authority. The horrid sense of something alien and undiscoverable beyond receives its quietus. There is, the inspired philosopher asserts, always something beyond the known, but it is always a repetition of what he has discovered: it is this again and again. And so without further exploration, and without the super-human labour of changing his habitual categories, the philosopher realises his dream of finding the trope, vast or minute, which nature shall be condemned to exhibit for ever.

Notion of recurrent cycles.

To assume such inertia in things, when existence is essentially inventive and spirit the most sublimated and volatile form of it, might seem to be itself a curious instance of inertia: and of inertia in the wrong place, because thought at least might be lively. But the motive and the true sphere for such a love of finality lie in the moral life; there it is indeed imperative to find a master trope, and to stick to it. The psyche (as we shall see presently) is herself a trope, not a substance: but a trope so imbedded in substance as to execute itself energetically, when it has a chance, and not merely to be exhibited passively, by a concourse of other tropes. The psyche is a definite potentiality rooted in a seed, and exhibited unswervingly in the development of that seed, if suitably nourished and allowed to mature. Such an innate but merely potential trope, which an animal strives to realise by his growth and action, has the aspect of a will; it may become conscious: not at first or normally conscious of its own ultimate form, but rather of incidental contrasts between pleasure and pain, success and failure, involved in the realisation of its destiny. In hunger and the chase, in wounds and constraint, an animal gradually learns to distinguish such objects and actions as are good, in that they further the discharge of his innate powers, from such as thwart this discharge and are evil. All experience and wisdom will do nothing but define for him the trope in which his life moves or ought to move; hence the profound marriage of animal life with reason, with definition, with selection. Hence, too, the abusive projection in human philosophy of rules of art upon the flux of existence. The realm of matter, for the moralised spirit, seems to exist only to be mastered, to be reformed, to be painted. Such is indeed its moral function in man, in so far as he profits by its economy. Profit, or the hope of it, rules the thrifty mind, not only in religion, where the edifying

Moral justification of the demand for fixity.

aspect of things is deputed to be their essence, but also in science, where the most august philosophers, in order to judge between true and false theories, often employ the childish criterion of simplicity. The flux, however, is not subject to these subjections; and only a speculative spirit, after much discipline, can learn to rejoice with it in its freedom.

CHAPTER VII

TELEOLOGY

WE have already seen that explanation by habit or law is a reduction of events to their rhythms or repetitions; we gain no insight into why or how a thing happens by saying that it has often happened before. Did we really wish to understand, we should inquire into the inner elements of such a mutation in any one of its instances: because a thing must happen each time by a concourse of motions there, and not because the same thing happens also in other places; although naturally it will happen again if the conditions which produced it here are repeated. Now a different form of mock explanation appears in what is called teleology, when the ground of things is sought in their excellence, in their harmony with their surroundings, or in the adaptation of organs to their functions and of actions to their intentions.

Like explanation by law, explanation by purpose is verbal only.

Such correspondences exist: teleology, if it be only a name for them, is a patent and prevalent fact in nature. Indeed the adaptation of things to one another is involved in their co-existence: a thing can arise only by finding and taking its place where other things make room for it. Everything in the moving equilibrium of nature is necessarily co-operative. But the question becomes interesting (and unanswerable) when we ask why, at any point, this

Nature a web of adaptations.

so singular thing should have found such a singular
set of conditions as to permit or compel it to exist there.
A wider view, exploring antecedents and consequents,
and discovering analogies, may enlarge the prospect,
and, as happens in the books of naturalists, may so
pleasantly occupy the mind with pictures and stories,
that we may stop asking for reasons. And to invoke
adaptation itself, as if this were a cause of adaptation,
would be to halt at a word, adding perhaps to it, as an
element of power, the bated breath with which we
pronounce it.

Yet this human scale and these human emotions,
which we impose so fatuously on the universe, bear
witness, on the plane of thought, to the existence of
organisms and of life on the plane of matter; for we
should have no emotions and no scale to impose on
other things if our own being were not definite, animate,
and self-assertive.

In human society teleology takes a special and
conscious form: it becomes art. Not only do tropes—
which here we call methods—everywhere   Might art
dominate the scene, but very often the method be the key
is explicitly adopted or modified, and the   to nature?
action planned; foresight and intention occupy the
first moment of it, and execution of that prevision
occupies the second moment. Here the preformation
of events and the pre-adaptation of instruments to
their uses is a simple fact of history. Knowing how
our passions and purposes watchfully realise their
avowed ends, may we not reasonably assimilate obscure
events to these deliberate actions, the causes of which
seem clear to us and intimately confessed? As we do
things when we wish, must not all nature, or God
working through nature, wish everything when they
do it? Must not some idea, seen under the form of
the good, guide and attract every movement in nature?

Yes: that is the normal way of speaking, the

rhetorical or poetical way of describing nature in human terms from the human point of view. But moral

Yes, but only in the realm of art. sentiment, poetry, and theology are forms of literature, not of science; they are not wrong in their own sphere, and their rightness becomes intelligible, and takes its place in natural history, when we see its relativity to human experience, and its psychic seat. There, in literature, a sceptic should be the last to quarrel with the use of moral analogies in describing nature: poetry does not contradict science, because in daring to be poetry, it avows a complete ignorance and disdain of the prose of things. Poetry is poetry, and opens up a legitimate vista within its own world, but only to a poetic spirit; in its material existence it is a flood of verbiage incidental to human passions and their rhetorical automatisms. In its biological capacity poetry can be described only in prose; and all its insights reappear as incidents and as subjective creations bred in the realm of matter.

Before indicating, in the tentative way which alone is possible, the material basis of teleology, it may be

Moral being has physical roots and works only through them. well to examine the logic of it in the imagination; for the contrast between poetry and prose is by no means absolute, and any scrupulous study of moral philosophy compels us to restore that subject, and ourselves who pursue it, to our place in nature. The clearness of moral life after all is only a verbal clearness; a sort of facility and acceleration by which our acts and feelings come to a climax and fulfil their natural tropes. We are left in the dark concerning the manner of this fulfilment. We are even more in the dark as to the ground of the ideas and wishes which, as we say, guide our conduct; when all goes well, we need not stop to question them, but presently when they clash with one another and fail of fulfilment, the

easy miracle of their power begins to seem dubious,
and subterranean bonds between them and the world
of action become visible in a new, a biological, direction.
Consider first the existential presence of human
wishes and ideas. Is it conceivably an original fact
and unconditioned? Why should any wish *All wishes*
or idea arise at all here and now? Is the *and ideas*
mid-void peopled with them, as with little *physical*
winged heads of cherubs, without bodies and *occasions,*
without support? Surely if anything ever had a cause
and was evidently secondary, it is human will and fancy;
to take them for absolute beings, or original powers,
would be to allow theoretical sophistries to blind us
to the plainest facts. If I want water, it is because
my throat is parched; if I dream of love, it is because
sex is ripening within me. Nature has fixed the character, and circumstances have fixed the occasion, for
this ferment of desire and conception. Conscious will
is a symptom, not a cause; its roots as well as its consequences are invisible to it, material, and often incongruous and astonishing.

But suppose that the mind, like some morose tyrant,
determines to shut all doors and windows against the
outer world, and to see only by the lamp of *and*
self-consciousness. What will be the stuff *physical*
of its meditations? Nothing but animal *objects.*
wishes and barn-yard ideas; demands for food, air,
liberty of motion; dreams of wild things to be chased,
eaten, played with, or hidden; or perhaps of fame to be
won, empires conquered, friendship and love and praise.
How comes absolute free-will or a groundless moral
energy to choose these singular objects? Could it
not have employed its inviolable leisure and its infinite
invention in conceiving something better than such
a very humble, cruel, and nasty animal world? And
could not its sentiment have been less sentimental,
less unctuous and constrained, less tainted by terror

and desperate delusion? Why are human love and
religion so tormented, if they are masters of the world?
If they command miraculously and matter obeys, is
it not because matter had first created them and dictated the commands which they were to issue?

Evidence of this, if it were needed, might also
be found in the loose character of ideas and wishes
They are   compared with their fulfilments, even when
inadequate   they are materially fulfilled. These ideas and
feelings
accompany- wishes are personal, confused, and incom-
ing action. plete. When a law-giver designs a constitution or an architect an edifice, a thousand contrary
principles and suggestions assault his mind. Unless
he is very precipitate, or an absolute slave of habit, the
plan will take shape in his mind to his own surprise;
it will be a sudden concretion of subtle currents and
accidents within him, the harmony and relevance of
which, if any, we call his genius or his ability. Even
when these are greatest, and most seasoned by experience, their prophetic virtue will be only abstract
and partial; the event will be a new surprise, as was the
idea. For it is hardly possible that the edifice when
complete, or the constitution when in actual operation,
should produce the same impression on the mind as
the plan conceived there originally. The plan arose
by a synthesis of acquired impulses within one body:
the work arises by a concourse of actions which, even
if still those of the same person only, and obedient to
the same vital impulses as the idea (as happens in
singing, speaking, or making a gesture) yet occur now
in the outer world, in a comparatively foreign material,
and with a greater admixture of accidental concomitants.
Therefore a man's actions and works seem to him less
a part of himself than his intentions, but to others seem
more so: because to others he is a personage and to
himself he is a mind.

Ideas and wishes, then, are mental echoes of movements proper to bodily life; were they not, they could have no application and no relevance to the world. The more accurately they prefigure events and seem to control them by prescribing their tropes, the better they prove their own fidelity to the ruling impulses of matter. Clear ideas are evidences of clean arts; a firm and victorious will bears witness to a strong and opportune economy in the organism. *Scientific psychology itself is a study of behaviour, i.e. of matter.* Indeed, for a scientific psychology behaviour is the only conceivable seat of mind, and intelligence simply a certain plasticity in organisms which enables them to execute tropes in subtle harmony with their material opportunities. True, mind and intelligence are something more in fact. This we perceive when, in reflection, we gather up sensuous images, memories, lyric effusions, and dramatic myths into a literary psychology, which may be remarkably convincing but remains purely literary; for it cannot follow the flux of its subject-matter by observation and measurement, but must recreate it in imagination, and leave it at that. Similarly, the history which interweaves intentions with events and ideas with motions may give a capital description of moral perspectives, but it is simply literature.

Total events in nature are never wholly mental, and it is on their material side, through their substance and physical tensions, that they are derived from previous events and help to shape the events which follow. But this doctrine is based on far-reaching considerations which may often be ignored; and when only the *Mental events, if causal, would not be teleological.* mental side of an event is discovered, the material and substantial side of it may be denied, and states of mind, in their purity, may be regarded as total natural events. It will then seem plausible to regard them as links in the chain of natural causes, for are they not moments in experience, as memory or dramatic reconstruction may survey it? But this amphibious psycho-physics, even if we admitted it, would not be teleological. Each mental event would transmit existence and energy to its successor in proportion to its own intensity and quality, just as if it were a form of matter. It would not thereby exercise any magical moral control over its consequences. Thus intense thought might make the head ache, fear might cause paralysis, amusement laughter, or love a want of appetite and early death. The teleological virtue of wishes and ideas is accordingly something quite distinct from their alleged physical influence; indeed it is only when we disregard this incongruous mechanical efficacy attributed to them that we begin to understand what their teleological virtue would mean: it would mean a miraculous pre-established harmony between the commands or wishes of the spirit and events in the world. It would mean the exercise of divine power, which a well-advised human being could never attribute to himself, but only to the grace of God, perhaps passing through him.

Teleology then retreats into a theology, or into a cosmological idealism, fraught with curious alternatives: The will for a divine mind, if conscious and omniscient invoked, as high theology would make it, would not be if cosmic, an event; it would be a decree, a command- would be ment, or an eternal glory relative to all events, mythical. but on a different plane from any of them. If, on the contrary, the divine will was immanent in the world and intermingled with all natural events, it would evidently not be separate or self-conscious; indeed, it would be only a poetic synonym for the actual fertility of matter, and for the tropes exhibited in its evolution. In either case, after making our bow to this divine will, out of deference to antiquity and to human rhetoric, we should be reduced to studying as far as possible the crawling processes of nature. These will be the seat of such teleology as surely exists, and as a critical philosophy may record without falling into rhetorical ambiguities. Organic life is a circular trope which at each repetition touches or approaches a point which we regard as its culmination, and call maturity. In man, maturity involves feelings, intentions, and spiritual light: but it is idle to regard the whole trope as governed by these top moments in it, which are more highly conditioned, volatile, and immaterial than are their organs, their occasions, or their fruits.

Nature is full of coiled springs and predestined rhythms; of mechanisms so wound up that, as soon as circumstances permit, they unroll themselves through a definite series of phases. A seed, if suitable sown and watered, will grow into one particular sort of plant, and into no other. At the inception of such a trope the predestined movement is said to be "potential"; there is a " predisposition " in matter at that point to execute the whole movement. What is this predisposition? Examination of a seed would probably never disclose in it a perfect model of the future flower, any more than examination of a young man's passions, or of his body, would disclose there the poems which these passions might ultimately inspire. Potentiality seems to be an imputed burden, a nominal virtue attributed to the first term of a trope because of the character of the rest of it. Yet, sometimes, as in a seed, the imputed burden is genuine, and potentiality is pregnancy. A true beginning and sufficient cause of what ensues is really found there; but this initial reality need not at all resemble that which it will become. Its nature is internal, hidden, perhaps inexpressible in the terms of human observation at all; so far is it from being an image cast into that well from the outside, or a reflex name given to it in view of the future. The tropes which mark the obvious metres of nature tell nothing

There is an untraced pregnancy in organic matter.

of the inspiration, the secret labour, or the mechanism which brings them forth.

Heredity is an obvious case of repetition; but its temporal scale is so large in respect to an observer of his own species that individualities may seem to him more striking and self-grounded than uniformities. Yet from a little distance, or in an alien species, heredity recedes into a monotonous succession of waves and a multitudinous repetition of objects. Both impressions are just, and nature, here seen at close quarters, reveals the complexity of her endless pulsations. There is a curious involution of the organism in the seed. The seed is not merely the first state of the organism in the offspring but was also a part of a similar organism in the parent. This notable trope is apt to blind us to the mechanism requisite for its repetition. We are solicited by the magic rhyme of it to rest content with explaining the beginning of life by the end, the part by the whole, the actual by the ideal, the existent by the non-existent. Abandoning physics altogether as incapable of solving the mystery, we may wonderingly record the reappearance, by the will of God, of new generations of every species, each after its kind. But as in the Christian sacraments, so here in natural reproduction, the grace of God does not operate without physical continuity in its channels; and it would be by tracing that continuity, and the accidents which often cause it to deviate from its course, that reproduction might be seen in its natural setting. The multitude of successes would not then blind us to the far greater number of failures. To arise in this world and to become something specific is in each instance a fresh and doubtful undertaking.

Prodigious complexity is something to which nature is not averse, like a human artist, but on the contrary is positively prone; and in animals the attainment of

[marginal note:] Heredity is a trope revealing the separate and perilous realisation of its instances.

such prodigious complexity is made possible by the fact that a special environment is at hand, in the body of the parent, enabling the young organism to run through its earlier and fundamental phases safely, surely, and quickly. So unerring is this development that the animal is often born complete; yet there is enough wavering, with false starts in directions once taken by the species and since abandoned, to show that the core of the seed need contain no prefigurement of the whole result, but that this result is reached tentatively in reproduction, as it was originally in evolution; only that the ovum is a far better locus for a perfect development of the psyche than was the bleak outer world.

Nevertheless the manner of this quick and spontaneous growth is little understood, and only the total trope remains to furnish our imagination. Seeing its dramatic unity, we feel that the first term must be pregnant with the ultimate issue, as the first act of a good play—assuming human nature and the ways of the world—is pregnant with the last. We forget that poetic genius itself must have natural sources and reason external guides; and we attribute the perpetual attainment of some natural perfection to the miraculous power of the trope realised in it, or to the divine will contemplating that trope and, as if fascinated by its magic beauty, commanding matter to reproduce it for ever and ever.

Final causes certainly exist in the conduct of human beings, yet they are always inadequate to describe the events in which they are manifested, since such events always presuppose a natural occasion and a mechanical impulse; and these cannot flow from the purpose or choice which they make possible and pertinent. The whole operation of final causes therefore requires, beneath and within it, a deeper flow of natural forces which we may darkly assign to fate or matter or chance or the unfathomable will of God. Yet, since without

Final causes exist, but are moral perspectives superposed on natural causation.

this irrational occasion or afflatus those purposes and choices could never have taken shape, it ought to suffice for our reasonable satisfaction if, in some measure, the natural perfections of things are manifested in them, and if there is some degree of harmony between the world and the spirit. Moral tropes have their proper status and dignity if they are actually found in the human aspect of events; they are not rendered false or nugatory merely because the material existence pre-supposed in them has a different method of progression. Medicine and psychology are now disclosing a truth which men of experience have perceived in all ages, that virtues and vices are equally phases of a controllable physical life: a fact which takes nothing away from their beauty or horror. They are the moral qualities of a natural being.

Mechanical tropes in their turn are incompetent to describe or measure spiritual realities, such as excellence or happiness or spirit itself; nor is it reasonable to require them to do so. They will be amply authenti-cated if they can serve to trace the whole material back-ing and occasions of those moral harmonies or spiritual lights. These, in order to arise do not require a different mechanism of their own, or a different occasion; the material mechanism and the material occasion fully suffice to introduce and to justify them. The physical terror of murder has made murder criminal; the animal warmth and transport of love have made love tender and deep. Of course, a deepening of apprehension is required, founded itself on a changed habit, a finer involution of responses in the organism; so that the same things which were done and regarded brutally may be done and regarded with a far-reaching sense of all that they involve. This new sense sees light and glow in the fire, of which the blinder senses could feel only the heat. Hence if either the naturalist or the moralist is a man of a single sense he must be left to grope in his professional half-light. Nature in his children will probably redress the balance.

The fact that natural organisms are far more closely purposeful than works of art, may itself serve to reveal the true superposition of art upon nature. Art is a human, marginal, not indispensable extension of natural teleology. The essential organic tropes, passions, and powers of man must have been first firmly rooted in the race, before anyone could conceive a project, or be able to execute it as conceived. Even highly civilised humanity forms its plans only dreamfully, and is cheated by its own impotence, or by contrary currents, in the execution of them. Often the most fixed purposes and the most vehement efforts are wasted; indeed, they are always wasted in some measure, because no designer can foresee all the circumstances of his work, or its ulterior uses. Any work, when it exists, is a part of the realm of matter, and has its fortunes there, far from all control or intention. The saintly Henry the Sixth founded Eton and King's College for the salvation of souls; they have served admirably together with the playing-fields to form the pensive but quite earthly ethos of the modern Englishman. In the works of nature there is not this division, nor this irony; the uses are not forecast in any purpose, consciously prophetic; they are simply the uses which the thing finds or develops, as it changes under the control of the changing circumstances. Thus the precision of adjustment between organs and functions, far from being a miracle, is in one sense a logical necessity or tautology; since nothing has any functions but those which it has come to have, when plasticity here with stimulus and opportunity there have conspired to establish them.

An organism is a concretion in matter which can feed, defend, and reproduce itself. Its initial form of expansion finds a natural limit, beyond which circum-

Art is a marginal imperfect form of natural organisation.

K

stances do not suffer it to go: then, unless it perishes altogether, it reproduces itself: that is, it breaks up into parts, some of which repeat the original form of expansion, while the others dissolve into their elements and die. Expansion thus becomes rhythmical, repeating a constant trope; except that, if the force of concretion and accretion is powerful at that centre, and if the circumstances are favourable, that trope may become internally more complex: in other words, the organism may acquire fresh organs. These will reappear in each generation in their due place and season, if the environment continues to give them play; and in this way a race and a species will be established, individual and recognisable, yet subject to private variations and also to generic shifts, by the atrophy of some organs and the development of others.

Brief natural history of organisms.

If, then, we understood genesis we should understand heredity; for an organ cannot arise, either the first time or the last, except spontaneously, and as if it had never existed before. But how can it arise at all? By what genetic impulse does some nucleus of matter modify its parts, and complicate their sympathetic movements, without losing its unity of action in respect to external things? It is for the naturalists to reply, in so far as observation or experiment enables them to trace the actual genesis of bodies; for as to the verbal explanations which they may offer, they are not likely to be on the scale or in the terms proper to the flux or to the concretions of matter at a depth so far below that of human language. Let matter take shape as it will: all that concerns me here is the nature of the teleology present in the result. Organs must arise before they can exercise what we call their function, and this function must be one which the circumstances usually render possible and self-maintaining. Is the philosopher reduced to impressions

Need final causes be operative to form them?

on the human scale? Must he blankly confess that nature is mysteriously inspired, and that matter gathers itself into organisms as if it were magically guided by the love of that life and those achievements of which such organisms will be capable?

Not quite. Moralistic physics is wiser than natural science in not ignoring eventual spiritual issues; but these issues are no factors in generation. On the contrary, they are themselves uncertain, conditioned, and precarious; so that if we reach any depth or honesty in our reflection *No: because purposes presuppose organisms.* we cannot attribute the movement of nature to the antecedent influence of the future good which she might realise. Instead, we must attribute the pursuit of this good, and its eventual realisation, to her previous blind disposition, fortified by the fact that circumstances were favourable to that development: and this last fact is no accident, since (as we have just seen) the adaptation of the parts of nature to one another is necessary to their existence, and nature could not retain any disposition for which circumstances did not make room, at least for the moment. In a word, the teleology present in the world must be distinguished from final causes. The latter are mythical and created by a sort of literary illusion. The germination, definition, and prevalence of any good must be grounded in nature herself, not in human eloquence.

The conditions of existence, as I conceive it, involve change and involve adaptation: perhaps if we ponder these necessities we shall gain some insight into the origin of organisms and the secret of life. Each natural moment has a *Concretions arise inevitably in a flux of substance.* forward tension, it is a moment of transition. Its present quality was determined by the force of lateral tensions guiding the previous dynamic stress of its substance; and the issue, as this moment passes into the next, will be determined by the lateral tensions to which its inner or forward tension is now subject. Is it not then native and proper to existence in its primary elements to congregate and to roll itself together into shells fashioned by its seeds, and into seeds fostered by its climate? And will not this initial concretion at any point go on swallowing what it can, destroying what it must, and harmonising its own complexity, until some contrary wind or some inner exhaustion disperses its elements? May not this disruption itself become less frequent with the extension of any cosmos, and the better co-ordination of the motions within it? A natural moment may be prolonged or reiterated; it may be caught up in a trope itself indefinitely recurrent, so that associated moments, duly spaced and controlled by their mutual tensions, may for a long time reappear in a fixed order. Any trope will recur if within its substance, or near by, there is generated a fresh natural moment, like the original one, and under similar conditions. Nothing more is required for a swarming or a hereditary life to cover the face of nature.

Every natural moment, in which matter at any point holds some essence unchanged, is fit to be the seed of all creatures and the centre of all thought. Some sequels might be reached only by a great and prosperous development from that moment outward; others might require the dissolution of this complex, and a fresh beginning, in some other direction, from one of its radical elements. But forwards or backwards, everything might be arranged round any nucleus, without the least violence or suppression of its original life, if only it were planted in the requisite soil. This profound naturalness of the greatest complications becomes clear to us in health, when we move spontaneously and think smoothly; it is only in disease that we tremble at our own incredible complexity, and

All matter is fit to be the matter of anything, if circumstances draw it into that form.

that harmony becomes a problem. In fact harmony in
itself is neither more difficult nor rarer than disorder:
that which demands a rare concourse of circumstances
is harmony *of this sort, here*; and yet, in the special
circumstances in which anything arises, harmony with
that thing is presupposed, otherwise that particular
thing would not have arisen. When our own ready-
made being and action are the facts in the foreground,
we instinctively and justifiably take it for granted that
surrounding nature is in harmony with them and will
give them suitable play; they are not unconditioned
or omnipotent, but they are co-operative with their
world. It is only when a different harmony, not native
to us, is suggested, that it seems to us impossibly
difficult of attainment and, if actual, miraculous.
Before we could adapt our presumptions and impulses
to that alien order we should need to retrace our steps
and follow that other path of development. Everything that is, except where it is, would be infinitely
improbable.

Thus the very fluidity of the flux, in its moving
equilibrium, causes every concretion that can arise to
arise, and every organism to maintain itself
which can maintain itself. Such is the Repetition
and varia-
feeble yet ineradicable sympathy in the poor tion flow
heart of matter towards the whole realm of indifferently
from the
essence. With many a false start, with a same
principle.
momentum and an organic memory often
disastrous, with an inertia always trustfully blind,
existence passes inevitably and in many streams from
what it is to what it can be; it changes in the very act
of continuing, and undermines its condition in surrounding it with developments and supports. Then,
when any of these concretions collapses, as they must
all collapse in turn, it returns to the charge, perhaps
in the same direction, like Sisyphus, or like Proteus,
in quite another. In the first case we speak of repro-

duction, in the second of evolution: but these words do not stand for different forces or principles but only for different results. In reproduction the flux repeats the same trope, in evolution it changes that trope for one more complex or appropriate, imposed by a new balance of forces.

That collapse is inevitable follows from the fact that existence is essentially chaotic. Its parts, perhaps infinite in multitude, will be always readjust- *Enough for the day is the good thereof.* ing their mutual tensions, so that, ultimately, the ground gives way under any edifice. And the catastrophe may ruin more than that confident system; it may radically transmute the elements which composed it, since every essence which matter may wear is arbitrary and, if occasion offers, may be exchanged for some other. Moreover, any trope has limits. The matter which executes or re-produces it, having done so, falls back into the relative chaos which remains the background of everything; so that death, in every instance, is the end of life; and in nature at large death can be only temporarily and imperfectly circumvented by fertility. I speak of fertility in a particular species and within one moral world: for of new creations there is presumably no end, and one perfection can neither remember nor desire another.

I confess that the life of the spider, or my own life, is not one which, if I look at it as a whole, seems to me worth realising; and to say that God's ways are not our ways, and that human tastes and scruples are impertinent, is simply to perceive that moral values cannot preside over nature, and that what arises is not the good, in any prior or absolute sense, but only the possible at that juncture: a natural growth which as it takes form becomes a good in its own eyes, or in the eyes of a sympathetic poet. Then this good realised endows with a relative and retrospective excellence all the conditions favourable to its being, as if with prophetic kindness and parental devotion they had conspired to produce it. The spider is a marvel of pertinacity, and I am not without affection for my own arts and ideas; we both of us heartily welcome the occasions for our natural activities; but when those occasions and activities have passed away, they will not be missed.

CHAPTER VIII

THE PSYCHE

OF all tropes the most interesting to the moralist is that which defines a life, and marks its course from Life not birth to death in some human creature. But an effect a life is also the most crucial of tropes for the of spirit natural philosopher; for here his congenial agitating natural philosopher; for here his congenial matter. mathematical categories leave him in the lurch, and he must either recognise their inadequacy to express the intimate flux of substance, or else cut his world in two, appending a purely literary or moral psychology to his mathematical physics. If emotional life preoccupies him, and he cannot simply ignore it, he may even be tempted to revert to the most primitive of dualisms, and to conceive the flux of existence as the resultant of two opposite agents: one an inert matter only capable of sinking into a dead sea of indistinction: the other a supernatural spirit, intrinsically disembodied, but swooping down occasionally upon that torpid matter, like the angel into the pool of Bethesda, and stirring it for a while into life and shape.

Need I give reasons, after all that has preceded, Matter is, for discarding this last conception? In the by defini- first place it would be a materialistic and tion, the superstitious view of spirit to regard it as a principle superstitious view of spirit to regard it as a of all wind, an effort, or any kind of physical force. motions. On the other hand, in conceiving matter to be inert, merely heavy, and intrinsically blank, we should

136

be forgetting our original reason for positing matter at all; and instead of that existing substance, filling the field of action, and necessarily fertile in everything to be encountered there, we should be considering some casual symbol for matter, such as ignorant sensation or abstract science may have created. To say that matter, as it truly exists, is inert or incapable of spontaneous motion, organisation, life, or thought, would be flatly to contradict the facts: because the real matter, posited in action, and active in our bodies and in all other instruments of action, evidently possesses and involves all those vital properties.

Nevertheless, the venerable tradition which attributes the fashioning of the body to the soul might be retained, if only we could restore to the word "soul" all its primitive earthliness, potency, and mystery. Soul, as often in antiquity, would then signify an animating current widely diffused throughout the cosmos, a breath uncreated and immortal as a whole, but at each point entering some particular body and quitting it, in order to mingle again with the air, the light, the nether darkness, or the life of the god from which it came. Such a warm, fluid, transmissible agent would evidently be material. Industry requires hands: a traceable cause of specific motions must travel through space in particular channels. And indeed, that the soul was material, was once taken for granted both in India and in Greece. On the other hand, the Platonic and Christian tradition has come to identify the soul with a bodiless spirit, a sort of angel, at first neglecting and afterwards denying the biological functions which were the primitive essence of the soul; until in modern times the soul has been discarded altogether and its place taken by consciousness, something which in reality is the last and most highly conditioned of the works of a natural soul.

A soul moulding the body would be itself material.

Thus a soul or an angel became, for the Christian imagination, a supernatural substance, a personal spirit *Christian* without material organs, yet somehow still *notion of* capable of seeing, loving, and thinking, and *the soul.* even of exercising physical force and making its presence felt in particular places. In man, and perhaps in other creatures, an evil fate had imprisoned some of these angelic souls in a natural body, and contaminated them with the vital principle—the old animal heathen soul—proper to such a body. Sometimes, under the influence of Aristotle and of the Apostolic doctrine of the resurrection of the flesh, theologians have endeavoured to bridge the chasm between these two souls, one generative and the other degenerate. Thus the orthodox Catholic doctrine declares that by a special act of creation a rational immortal soul, previously non-existent, is substituted during gestation for the animal soul of the embryo: the new supernatural soul taking on the functions of the previous natural soul in addition to its own, and by that union becoming subject to their influence; an influence which marks the fallen state of the supernatural soul and its participation in the sin of Adam. A forced conjunction of two incompatible beings is obvious here, yet this conjunction is not without its dramatic propriety in expressing theoretically the moral conflicts of the Christian life; and the same incongruities reappear in any doctrine which would make the soul immaterial and its functions physical. A soul essentially generative and directive must be capable of existing unconsciously and of exerting material energy. If it were ever clearly identified with consciousness it would evaporate into a passing feeling or thought, something unsubstantial, volatile, evanescent, non-measurable and non-traceable. Once recognised in its spiritual actuality, this thought would not only be obviously incapable of exercising the vegetative and propulsive functions of animal life, but would loudly call for such an animal life to support its own intuitions and lend them their place in nature and their moral significance.

Avoiding, then, this poetical word, the soul, laden with so many equivocations, I will beg the reader to distinguish sharply two levels of life in the human body, one of which I call *the spirit*, and the other *the psyche*. By spirit I understand the actual light of consciousness falling upon anything—the ultimate invisible emotional fruition of life in feeling and thought. On the other hand, by the psyche I understand Definition a system of tropes, inherited or acquired, of the displayed by living bodies in their growth psyche. and behaviour. This psyche is the specific form of physical life, present and potential, asserting itself in any plant or animal; it will bend to circumstances, but if bent too much it will suddenly snap. The animal or plant will die, and the matter hitherto controlled by that psyche will be scattered. Such a moving equilibrium is at once vital and material, these qualities not being opposed but coincident. Some parcels of matter, called seeds, are predetermined to grow into organisms of a specific habit, producing similar seeds in their turn. Such a habit in matter is a psyche.[1]

In literary psychology the psychic often means simply the mental; and the reader may be disconcerted by the suggestion that the truly psychic, the dynamic life of both body and mind, is on the contrary material. Let me remind him, in that case, of the following fundamental points:

1. The psyche is not another name for consciousness or mind. Everything truly conscious or mental—feeling, intuition, intent—belongs to the realm of spirit. We may say of spirit, but not of the psyche, that its essence is to think. The psyche is a natural fact, the fact that

_____
[1] A further illustration of this definition of the psyche may be found in my *Soliloquies in England*, pp. 217-224.

many organisms are alive, can nourish and reproduce themselves, and on occasion can feel and think. This is not merely a question of the use of words: it is *a deliberate refusal to admit the possibility of any mental machinery*. The machinery of growth, instinct, and action, like the machinery of speech, is all physical: but this sort of physical operation is called psychical, because it falls within the trope of a life, and belongs to the self-defence and self-expression of a living organism. How should any unsophisticated person doubt that the movements of matter have the nature of matter for their principle, and not the nature of spirit?

2. By the word matter I do not understand any human idea of matter popular or scientific, ancient or recent. Matter is properly a name for the actual substance of the natural world, whatever that substance may be. It would therefore be perfectly idle, and beside the point, to take some arbitrary idea of matter and to prove dialectically that from that idea none of the consequences follow with which the true substance of the world is evidently pregnant. What would be thereby proved would not be that matter cannot have the developments which it has, but that that particular idea of matter was wrong or at least inadequate.

3. In calling the psyche material I do not mean to identify her with any piece or kind of substance, an atom or monad or ether or energy. Perhaps all sorts of substances may enter into her system; she is not herself a substance, except relatively to consciousness, of which her movements and harmonies are the organ and the immediate support. She is a *mode* of substance, a trope or habit established in matter; she is made of matter as a cathedral is made of stone, or the worship in it of sounds and motions; but only their respective forms and moral functions render the one a cathedral or a rite, and the other a psyche.

4. The whole life of the psyche, even if hidden by

chance from human observation, is essentially observable: it is the object of biology. Such is the only scientific psychology, as conceived by the ancients, including Aristotle, and now renewed in behaviourism and psycho-analysis. This conception of the psyche also allows the adepts of psychical research to retain a congenial name for the very real region, far removed from everything that I call spiritual, in which occult processes, unusual powers, and subtle survivals may be actually discovered.

Biology aspires to be a part of physics, and this for the best of reasons, since in describing the spontaneous tropes that prevail in the flux of matter, physics is simply biology universalised. The problem is not where to place the frontier between two disparate regions, but only to discover how the tropes most obvious in each of them are superposed or grow out of one another. The inanimate world must needs concern the zoologist, since it pervades and unites all living creatures; and the animate world must needs concern the physicist, since it is the crown of nature, the focus where matter concentrates its fires and best shows what it is capable of doing. Obviously, if we could understand the inmost machinery of motion we should understand life, which on the biological level is simply a system of motions.

Continuity of physics and biology.

In one sense, indeed, all matter is alive. Its deadest principles, like gravity and inertia, are principles of motion. The dry dust and the still waters which the wind sweeps into a vortex, if mingled, will breed. Even celestial matter, which might seem too tenuous and glowing to be alive after our fashion, is fertile in light, which may be, perhaps, the primary stimulus to life, or a first form of it. Yet this universal ethereal trepidation is too diffuse and elusive to seem life to our human judgment, accustomed as we are to the crude contrast

Not all the energies of matter are properly vital or psychic.

between a barking dog and a dead one. Even in animals and plants the life in which, so to speak, nature is interested, the life which is transmitted and preserved, is not their individual life, describable in a biography. Its vegetative continuity takes a course which, from our point of view, seems subterranean and unfriendly; for it does not pass from one complete animal or plant to the next (as the phases of each life succeed one another for the observant spirit), but the child buds at mid-branch, and the tree obdurately outlives its seeded flowers. In fact, individuality and tenacity never are more pronounced than in that old age which, as far as the life of nature is concerned, is so much dead wood and obstructive rubbish. Life at our level has adopted a vehicle which—like all natural vehicles —has a form and a story of its own, apart from the inherited movement which it serves to propagate. The individual has outgrown his character of a mere moment in a flux; his trope is not simply the general trope repeated and passed on. It has become a redundant trope, surrounding that other with epicycles and arabesques and prolongations useless to the march of transmissible life, yet enriching it at its several stations.

It is only metaphorically, therefore, that the general movement of nature can be called a life, or said to be animated by a cosmic psyche. Nor would There is no cosmic soul. the attribution of these tropes to the universe as a whole explain why they should arise again within it. On the contrary, it is more natural to find fish in the sea than within other fishes. We may rather say that matter, although perhaps everywhere organic or at least ready to be organised, becomes animate only when it forms hereditary organisms; and that a psyche exists only in bodies that can assimilate and redistribute the substances suitable for preserving and propagating their type. Thus the cosmos—not feeding or breeding—can have no psyche, but only psyches within it; and the spirit is no psyche, but always has some psyche beneath, which sustains it.

Embryology, the most obscure part of biology, is accordingly the fundamental part of it. In the present state of knowledge, the psychologist is con- Profound demned to taking summary and superficial obscurity views of his subject, for he sees gross results, psychic gross variations, gross repetitions, and all the mechanism. fine, individual, intricate labour of the psyche escapes him. Physiology and organic chemistry work only with ready - made materials, which already possess inexplicable specific virtues and habits; and psycho-analysis, in really opening a trap-door, as disease does, into the dim carpentry of the stage, is compelled to transcribe that intricacy into metaphors. Its reports come to it in hectic language, the latest, most wayward, most hypocritical ebullition of psychic life; while its own theories, for lack of physiological knowledge, must be couched in mythological terms. Thus the psyche remains a mystery in her intrinsic operations; and if something of that mystery seems to hang about the feminine name we are giving her, so much the better: we are warned that we do not, and probably cannot, understand.

What our knowledge of the psyche lacks in precision it makes up, after a fashion, in variety and extent. All that is called knowledge of the world, of human nature, of character, and of the pas- The psyche, sions is a sort of auscultation of the psyche; like other and the familiarity of our verbal and dramatic natural mechanisms, conventions often blinds us to their loose is known to application, and to our profound ignorance us by her fruits. of the true mechanism of life. Not knowing what we are, we at least can discourse abundantly about our books, our words, and our social actions; and these manifestations of the psyche, though peripheral, are faithful enough witnesses to her nature. She is that inner moving equilibrium from which these things radiate, and which they help to restore—the equilibrium by which we live, in the sense of not dying; and to keep us alive is her first and essential function. It follows naturally from this biological office that in each of us she is one, vigilant, and predetermined; that she is selfish and devoted, intrepid and vicious, intelligent and mad; for her quick potentialities are solicited and distracted by all sorts of accidents. She slept at first in a seed; there, and from there, as the seed softened, she distributed her organs and put forth her energies, always busier and busier in her growing body, almost losing control of her members, yet reacting from the centre, perhaps only slowly and partially, upon events at her frontiers. If too deeply thwarted her industry becomes distraction; and what we sometimes call her plan, which is only her propensity, may be developed and transformed, if she finds new openings, until it becomes quite a different plan. But against brutal obstacles she will struggle until death; that is, until her central control, her total equilibrium and power of recuperation, are exhausted. Her death may as easily occur by insurrection within her organism—each part of which is a potential centre on its own account—as by hostile action from outside.

I hardly venture to say more. To watch a plant grow, or draw in its leaves, to observe the animals in a zoological garden, is to gain some knowledge of the psyche; to study embryology or the nervous system or insanity or politics, is (or ought to be) to gain more: and every system of science or religion is rich in this sort of instruction for a critic who studies it in order to distinguish whatever may be arbitrary in it, based on human accidents, and without any but a psychic ground. All the errors ever made about other things, if we understand their cause, enlighten us about ourselves; for the psyche is at once the spring of curiosity and the ground of refraction, selection, and distortion in our ideas. Summary reaction, symbolisation, infection with relativity and subjective colouring begins in the senses and is continued in the passions; and if we succeed in removing, by criticism, this personal equation from our science of other things, the part withdrawn, which remains on our hands, is our indirect knowledge of the psyche.

Each man also has direct experience of the psyche within himself, not so much in his verbal thoughts and distinct images—which if they are knowledge at all are knowledge of other things—as in a certain sense of his personal momentum, a pervasive warmth and power in the inner man. As he thinks and acts, intent on external circumstances, he is not unaware of the knot of latent determinate impulses within him which respond to those circumstances. Our thoughts—which we may be said to know well, in that we know we have had them often before—are about anything and everything. We shuffle and iterate them, and live in them a verbal, heated, histrionic life. Yet we little know *why* we have them, or how they arise and change. Nothing could be more obscure, more physical, than the dynamics of our passions and dreams; yet, especially in moments of suspense or hesitation, nothing could be more intensely felt. There is the coursing of the blood, the waxing and waning of the affections, a thousand starts of smothered eloquence, the coming on of impatience, of invention, of conviction, of sleep. There are laughter and tears, ready to flow quite unbidden, and almost at random. There is our whole past, as it were, knocking at the door; there are our silent hopes; there are our future discourses and decisions working away, like actors rehearsing their parts, at their several fantastic arguments. All this is the psyche's work; and in that sense deeply our own; and our superficial mind is carried by it like

And also directly, though vaguely, by self-consciousness.

L

a child, cooing or fretting, in his mother's arms. Much of it we feel going on unmistakably within our bodies, and the whole of it in fact goes on there. But the form which belongs to it in its truly physical and psychic character, in its vital bodily tropes, is even less known to us than the mechanism of the heart, or that by which our nerves receive, transmit, and return their signals. The psyche is an object of experience to herself, since what she does at one moment or in one organ she can observe, perhaps, a moment later, or with another organ; yet of her life as a whole she is aware only as we are aware of the engines and the furnaces in a ship in which we travel, half-asleep, or chattering on deck; or as we are aware of a foreign language heard for the first time, perceived in its globular sound and gesticulation and even perhaps in its general issue—that all is probably a dispute about money—yet without distinguishing the words, or the reasons for those precise passionate outbursts. In this way we all endure, without understanding, the existence and the movement of our own psyche: for it is the body that speaks, and the spirit that listens.

The psyche is the self which a man is proud or ashamed of, or probably both at once: not his body in its accidental form, age, and diseases, from which he instinctively distinguishes those initial impulses and thwarted powers which are much more truly himself. And this is the self which, if he lives in a religious age, he may say that he wishes to save, and to find reviving in another world. Yet this self is far from being a stranger to the body; on the contrary, it is more deeply and persistently the essence of the body than is the body itself. It is human, male or female, proper to a particular social and geographical zone; it is still the fountain of youth in old age; it deprecates in a measure the actions and words which circumstances

She is the internal source of the organism and of its action.

may have drawn from it, and which (it feels) do it enormous injustice; and yet the words and actions which it might have wished to produce instead are all words and actions of the same family, slightly more eloquent in the same human language, slightly more glorious in the same social sphere. The psyche is so much of us, and of our works, as is our own doing.

Conflicts between the flesh and the spirit, between habit and idea, between passion and reason, are real conflicts enough, but they are conflicts be- *All moral* tween one movement in the psyche and *conflicts* another movement there. Hers is a compound *or dualisms are internal* life, moulded by compromise, and compacted *to her life.* of tentative organs, with their several impulses, all initially blind and mechanical. Rarely will any particular psychic impulse or habit move in sympathy with all the rest, or be unquestionably dominant. It follows that what in religion or in moral reflection we call the spirit is a precarious harmony. It is threatened by subject powers always potentially rebellious, and it necessarily regards them as wicked and material in so far as they do not conspire to keep its own flame vivid and pure. And yet the spirit itself has no other fuel. Reason is not a force contrary to the passions, but a harmony possible among them. Except in their interests it could have no ardour, and, except in their world, it could have no point of application, nothing to beautify, nothing to dominate. It is therefore by a complete illusion, though an excusable one, that the spirit denies its material basis, and calls its body a prison or a tomb. The impediments are real, but mutual; and sometimes a second nucleus of passion or fleshliness rises against that nucleus which the spirit expresses, and takes the name of spirit in its turn. Every virtue, and in particular knowledge and thought, have no other root in the world than the co-ordination of their organs with one another and with the material habitat. Certainly such a co-ordination could never arise except in a psyche: the psyche is another name for it: but neither could the psyche have any life to foster and defend, nor any instruments for doing so, if she were not a trope arising in a material flux, and enjoyed a visible dominance there more or less prolonged and extended.

Thus the first function of the psyche in the seed is to create the outer body. With every organ which she

Formation and variation of the psyche equally a resultant of material tensions.

brings forth she acquires a new office and a new type of life. These changes and developments are not devised and suggested to the psyche by some disembodied spirit, whispering in her ear. Were they not the natural continuation of her innate tensions she would be justified in regarding these promptings as deceits and snares of the devil. For from the point of view of the psyche (whose innate impulse is the arbiter of morals) every change of purpose is a change for the worse: either a vain complication or a hideous surrender. It is only lateral tensions, circumstances, external pressure, that can compel her to recast her habits and become, to that extent, a new psyche. Surrenders are indeed inevitable when the action for which the soul is ready happens to be impossible, or organs once agile are atrophied by disuse; and new acquisitions of function are inevitable too, when new occasions induce a different mode of action, and preserve and solidify it. The burden of the psyche is in this way continually lightened in one quarter and accumulated in another. If crippled at first by some loss, she may ultimately heal the wound (healing being one of her primary functions) and may live on with her residual equipment all the more nimbly. On the other hand she often hardens herself to some novel exertion which at first was forced and distracting, until that exercise becomes instinctive and necessary to her health and peace, so that it is performed with alacrity and sureness whenever an occasion occurs. Habituation tames the spirit, or rather kills it in one form and recreates it in another. This forced attention to instrumentalities, this awkwardness, which marks the acquisition of a new art, yields in time to love and mastery; and the spirit rises again from its troubles and threatened death to happiness and confidence.

At bottom, however, the whole psyche is a burden to herself, a terrible inner compulsion to care, to watch, to pursue, and to possess. Yet to evade this Her mission predestined career would be a worse fate; and is to the psyche is more terribly corroded and discharge an imposed tormented for not doing, than she would be burden. harassed in doing, or disappointed at having done. Original sin must be purged, the burden discharged, the message delivered. Happiness—for the surface of the psyche is normally happy—lies for her in jogging on without too much foresight or retrospect, along the middle way, exercising her central functions heartily, and reverting to them, as to hearth and home, from those gambler's losses or commitments into which she may be tempted. In this way she may healthfully deliver herself in a long life of her native burden, transmit the same in a healthful measure, and sleep in peace.

Sleep is in a manner the normal condition of the psyche, from which in her vegetative and somatic labours she never awakes, unless it be to suffer; and we may fancy that a sort of sub-soul or potential life sleeps, and will always sleep, in the universe of matter, ready to shape it, when opportunity occurs, into the likeness of all essence. Yet as this labour must be in time, and in some one of many alternative courses, the greater part of that sleeping psyche remains unoccupied, and the occupied part anxious and full of the fear of death: from which indeed she cannot escape except by falling asleep again and forgetting, but never really removing, the peril of a new birth.

To be completely mastered by the psyche makes the health, agility, and beauty of the body. This sort of virtue is common among the brutes. It would seem to suffice that a very potent psyche— one to which its matter completely submits— should have entrenched herself in the seed and should surround it later with outworks so staunch and perfect that no ordinary hazard will pierce or bend them. Unquestioning fidelity to type is always a marvel, a victory of form over matter, which delights the contemplative spirit. In fragile organisms, such as children or flowers, this fidelity seems to us an appealing innocence; but in hard-shell organisms, which attempt to resist change by force of rigidity, it seems rather stupid. Brave and proud the conservative psyche may be: she will not suffer minor accidents to distract her from her first vows and native intentions; but against major accidents she has no resource save a total death; and on earth she must be extraordinarily prolific to survive at all.

Completely determinate psyches are beautiful but not safe.

The peculiarity of the human psyche, on the contrary, is her great relative plasticity. I will not call it intelligence, because that presupposes a fixed good to to be attained, and invention only of new means of attaining it. A total plasticity, that for greater convenience consents to change its most radical direction, would hardly be life; its only assignable purpose would seem to be survival, and even this would be illusory, since the psyche that was to survive would have abdicated in doing so, and would have committed suicide. This the human soul is capable of doing, morally as well as physically, as we see in madness, in conversion, and in the wilder passions; but ordinarily her plasticity remains only a means to a native end, an incidental adjustment in the interests of the major radical passions, which remain supreme at the centre. Yet this alert human psyche, more intelligent than wise, often forgets the treasure locked in the citadel, and lives by preference in her own suburbs, in the outer organs of action and perception. She then becomes distracted, frivolous, loquacious; and we may doubt whether all this agitation and knowingness relieve her of her inner burden, or only add a dreadful fatigue to a profound dissatisfaction.

Nor is this all: friction at the periphery more or less recoils to the centre and modifies the organisation there. Changes of food, temperature, climate, and rhythm may extend to the very substance of the seed whence the next generation is to grow; so that the psyche transmitted is not always exactly similar to the psyche inherited. *Some adaptations extend to the germ.* In the history of the earth, the evolution and transformation of psyches must have gone on from the beginning; and this reconstruction, which in some directions seems to have come to a temporary end and produced stable types of animals, in the human race still continues at an unusual rate. Not so much in the body—unless we regard clothes and weapons as equivalents to fur and claws—but in the singular equipment with instruments by which modern man has surrounded himself, and in the management of which he lives. The changes are so rapid that we can observe and record them: something perhaps impossible and inconceivable to any psyche except the human.

All this may be studied and described behaviour-istically, as a chapter in natural history; yet we know that the psyche so occupied has an inner invisible experience, which under these circumstances becomes very complex. The eloquence of language, the multitude of sights and sounds, the keen edge of silent emotion compose a perpetual waking dream—a view *The feeling always involved in psychic life becomes in animals perception and in man thought.* of the world which is not a part of the world and which even in sleep continues and shifts fantastically in many a muted development. This unsubstantial experience, which is alone immediate, is nothing new or paradoxical in kind. The psyche is probably never unconscious; she always feels, in some vague emotional form, the inherent stress of her innumerable operations. Her maturing instincts have their false dawn in her mind; she warms and awakes for a moment at their satisfaction, and simmers pleasantly when replete. But external perception is a keener, more inquisitive form of attention; it is less interested in what is given æsthetically, or even in what might be given, than in the action of things upon one another and on our bodies. At the same time, perception cannot fail to supply us with images—products of the inner psyche, like the feelings of blind animals—which serve to name and to clothe in our poetic consciousness those external objects of her concern. These images and those feelings, together with the constant flow of unspoken words which we call thinking, compose a mental or inner life. Its moments, though probably intent on external material events, are yet directly but symptoms of psychic movements; so that it requires only a shift in apperception to transform all this immediate experience from active consideration of dubious external objects into a certain and accurate index to an internal psychic life.

Not that these moments of spirit, these mental notes and mental vistas, *are* the psychic life in question. They form a thin flux of consciousness, chiefly verbal in most of us, which in reflective moods becomes self-consciousness, recollection, autobiography, and literature: all only the topmost synthesis, or play of shooting relations, on the surface of the unconscious. In this capacity, however, as a mental symptom or expression, self-consciousness gives infallible renderings of the agitation beneath. We may therefore use it, in so far as we can recollect it or

Secondary or expressive nature of consciousness.

reconstruct it, to describe the psyche and her passions, just as we use the essences given in perception to describe pictorially those parts of the material world on which the organs of perception react.

Hence a second approach to a science of the psyche, this time not biological or behaviouristic, but personal, through memory and repeatable mental dis- Possibility course; and this imagination of imagination of literary may fill our whole lives, composing a dramatic, psychology. social, religious world in which we suppose ourselves to be living. Such a moral world, the world of humanism, need not mislead in practice the psyche that creates it. Sometimes she may become more interested in this play-world—in religion, landscape, fiction, and eloquence—than in her natural circumstances. Yet all her imaginative life is interfused with language and akin to language, so that it often becomes a convenient or indispensable transcript for the march of things on the human scale. It may be so disciplined and adjusted to facts as to compose history and literary psychology.

The two sorts of psychology, the scientific and the literary, are clearly distinguished by Aristotle where he says that anger is a name for two different Its relation things, anger being physically a boiling of the to the humours and dialectically a desire for revenge. science of Boiling of the humours would be an exterior the psyche. and gross effect of the total movement of the psyche, and the natural history of a passion is far more complicated and far-reaching than any such symptom; yet the boiling is on the same plane as the whole object of biology, on the plane of behaviour, and gives us a first glimpse of what anger is, substantially considered. On the other hand, " a desire for revenge " is a current verbal and dramatic expression for such a passion: this too is summary and might be elaborated in each case into an almost infinite network of motives, memories, likes and dislikes, and delicate juxtapositions of images and words; yet whatever figments we might substitute for the conventional terms " anger " or " desire " would be further literary figments, verbal or intuitive units formed and re-formed by the discoursing spirit, and non-existent in the realm of matter. For this reason the most adequate and confident knowledge of human nature, rendered in literary terms, as in novels and plays, or in the gossip of busybodies, covers only what might be called the reasoned element in life—although it is for the most part foolish at bottom. The same psychology remains helpless in the presence of all the radical passions and all the natural collocations of persons and events by which the life of mind is determined.

Literature and literary philosophy are nevertheless the most natural and eloquent witnesses to the life of the psyche. Literature is conserved speech, speech is significant song, and song is a pure overflow of the psyche in her moments of free play and vital leisure. And this overflow is itself double: biological and ontological. Biologically it resembles the exuberance of the psyche in all her well-fed and happy moments, in the gambols of young animals, the haughtiness of all accomplished strength, or the endless experimentation in colours, forms, and habits characteristic of the psyche in fashioning her strange menagerie of bodies. Yet the ontological overflow, the concomitant emergence of consciousness, alone seems to arrest the wonder, not to say the wrath, of philosophers; and they are so surprised at it, and so wrathful, that they are inclined to deny it, and to call it impossible. I have not myself such an intrinsic knowledge of matter as to be sure that it cannot do that which it does: nor do I see why the proudest man should be ashamed of the parents who after all have produced him. I am not tempted seriously to regard consciousness as the very essence of life or even of being. On the contrary, both my personal experience and the little I know of nature at large absolutely convince me that consciousness is the most highly conditioned of existences, an overtone of psychic strains, mutations, and harmonies; nor does its origin seem more mysterious to me than that of everything else.

Let us, in this important matter, go back to first principles. From the beginning it was in the very nature of existence to be involved in indirect commitments. Being transitive, anything existing is always in the act of becoming something which it was not, and yet which it was the sufficient cause for producing, according to those irresponsible impulses which animate *Change, concretion, dissolution, and variation are intrinsic to a flux.* its matter and predetermine its fate. The sequel is always spontaneous and, if we are not dulled by habit, seems miraculous; yet it is always natural, since no other development would have been more so, and some development was inevitable. Nature is not that realm of essence where all variety and all relations are perspicuous and intrinsically necessary. Necessity, in nature, is only an irrational propulsion which, as a matter of fact, is prevalent; existence could not have begun to be, it could not have taken the first step from one form of being to another, if it had not been radically mad. But this madness not only has method in it—a method in itself arbitrary and doubtless variable —it has also a certain glorious profusion, a rising, cumulative intensity and volume, coming to a climax and then dying down. The flux thus runs inevitably into dramatic episodes, even in its own plane of matter; episodes in our eyes far more interesting than its general movement, which is perhaps only itself an episode in some more radical genesis of existence.

But the tacit commitments of such existence are not limited to the material plane. Every fact involves many a truth about it; it casts its shadow through infinite distances and makes relevant to it everything that it resembles and everything that it contradicts. By arising and by disappearing it introduces an unalterable event into history; it verifies or stultifies all prophecies concerning it and concerning the place which it fills in the context of nature, and which might have been filled otherwise; and it either justifies or renders false everything that anyone may say or think of it in future.

The eternal truth about it is also involved in it.

Here, then, is a whole infinite world, visible only to the intellect, but actually created and made precise by the blind flux of matter, whatsoever that flux may be. These are the indelible footprints which existence, thoughtlessly running on, neither knows nor cares that it is making, and which yet are its only memorial, its only redemption from death, the eternal truth about it.

Now, when the flux falls into the trope which we call a psyche, existence commits itself unawares to yet another complication; for now the reverberation of its movement in the realm of truth becomes, so to speak, vocal and audible to itself. Not indeed in its entirety—unless there be some divine sensorium to gather all its echoes together—but in snatches. At certain junctures animal life, properly a habit in matter, bursts as with a peal of bells into a new realm of being, into the realm of spirit. When does this happen, and how is this consciousness diversified and guided? We may presume that some slumbering sensibility exists in every living organism, as an echo or foretaste of its vital rhythms; and even when no assignable feeling comes to a head, if there is life at all, there is a sort of field of consciousness, or canvas spread for attention, ready to be occupied by eventual figures. Not by *any* figures, as if essences of their own initiative could come down and appear; but only by certain predetermined classes and intensities of sensation, possible to the particular

Where the flux is a psyche, some truths about it become occasions for feeling.

organs whose suspended animation, or busy growth, spreads that canvas and rings that ground-tone of potential feeling. When ambient influences or inner ripening modify this vital rhythm, or cause the psyche actively to assimilate or to repel that stimulant, organic slumber may easily awake to some special feeling or image. Thus sensations and ideas always follow upon organic reactions and express their quality; and intuition merely supplies a mental term for the animal reaction already at work unconsciously. With each new strain or fresh adjustment, a new feeling darts through the organism; digestive sleep breaks into moral alertness and sharp perception; and, once initiated, these modes of sensibility may persist even in quiescent hours —for they leave neurograms or seeds of habit in the brain—and may be revived in thought and in dreams.

Consciousness, then, in its genesis and natural status, is one of the indirect but inevitable outpourings proper to an existence which is in flux and gathers *Being* itself into living bodies. In consciousness the *spiritual in* psyche becomes festive, lyrical, rhetorical; she *essence, yet* caps her life by considering it, and talking to *conditioned,* herself about the absent parts of it. Con- *conscious-* sciousness is a spiritual synthesis of organic *ness can be* movements; and were it not this, no spirit and *knowledge* *of its source.* no consciousness would ever have any transcendent significance or any subject-matter other than the essences which it might weave together. Yet in fact, on account of its organic seat and material conditions, consciousness is significant. Its every datum is an index, and may become in its eyes a symbol, for its cause. In other words, consciousness is naturally cognitive. Its spiritual essence renders it an imponderable sublimation of organic life, and invisible there; yet it is attached historically, morally, and indicatively to its source, by being knowledge of it.

Thus, like truth, consciousness is necessarily faithful

to its basis in the flux of nature; it is a commentary on events, in the language of essence; and while its light is contemplative, its movement and intent strictly obey the life of the psyche in which it is kindled.

This knowledge is natural in its origin, validity, and scope.

Hence the whole assertive or dogmatic force of intelligence, by which the spirit ventures to claim knowledge of outspread facts, and not merely to light up and inspect a given essence. This whole extraordinary pretension rests on a vital compulsion, native to the body, imposing animal faith on a spirit in itself contemplative. For in animals the organs are inevitably addressed to intercourse with relevant external things, as well as to internal growth and reproduction. Suspense outwards, towards an object not within her organism, is habitual to the psyche. Her tentacles and her actions hang and grope in mid-air, like a drawbridge confidently let down to meet its appropriate ulterior point of contact and support. Even her vegetative life is prophetic, conscious of maturation, and rich in preparations for coming crises, vaguely prefigured but unhesitatingly pursued. Under such circumstances and with such organs, consciousness could not be pure intuition: it must needs be intuition carried by intent. The intent is adventurous; its object or ulterior development is hidden and merely posited. Yet by thus torturing itself, and uprooting itself from its immediate datum, spirit becomes perception, and perception knowledge, in ·all its transitive and realistic force. And this perception and knowledge are, for the same reason, normally and virtually true: not true literally, as the fond spirit imagines when it takes some given picture, summary, synthetic, and poetical, for the essence of the world; but true as language may be true, symbolically, pragmatically, and for the range of human experience in that habitat and at that stage in its history.

So much for the claims of spirit to possess knowledge,

and for the range of it. But whence the original qualities
of feeling itself, the choice of essences that shall
appear in intuition, the spectrum of each sense, *The*
the logic and grammar of each type of intelli- *spectrum*
gence? How does the psyche arrive at any *of sense*
of these creations, rather than at any other? *and the*
categories
Certainly out of her own substance, and by *of thought*
the natural diversity and fertility of the tropes *are original*
creations of
which she imposes on her own matter. The *the psyche.*
presumption of common sense, that these essences
belong in the first place to objects and pass from them
into the organs of sense, and somehow become evident
to spirit in the dark caverns of the brain, is unfortunately
untenable. We find it plausible—in spite of its in-
coherence and the many contrary facts—because we
begin our reflection at the end, armed with our working
conventions and dogmatic habits. We should readily
understand the enormous illusion involved, and the
false reduplication of our data, if we began at the
beginning, where in the natural world the psyche
begins. Surely pleasure and pain, hunger, lust, and
fear, do not first reside in external objects and pass
from them into the mind: and these are the primary,
typical data of intuition. All the rest—colours, sounds,
shapes, specious spaces and times and sensations of
motion—is hatched in the same nest; it all has a
similar psychic seat and dramatic occasion. If such
essences seem to be found in external things, it is for
the good and sufficient reason that outer things are
perceived by us in these sensible terms, and could not
be perceived were not the psyche sensitive, and fertile
in such signals to the spirit. All things might stand
facing one another for ever, clad in all the colours of
the rainbow; and were there no poetic psyche in any
of them, to turn those colours into feelings of colour
and intuitions of the soul, never would anything
perceive anything else.

The psyche is a poet, a creator of language; and there is no presumption that she will perceive material things, including her own substance and movement, at all in the terms or in the order and scale in which they exist materially. On the contrary, only the reactions of her organism are represented in her feelings; and these reactions, which are tropes subsisting only in the realm of truth, resemble in nothing the imponderable feelings which are involved in executing them. The fountain of sense and of sensible qualities lies indeed in the forward and inner tensions of natural moments, with their conjunctions and flow in a psyche. Pain, novel in essence, signalises a special nervous affection, not another pain elsewhere; and this signal is suitable, in as much as just such a cry would be uttered by any psyche in such a predicament, and for all psyches signifies predicaments of that sort. The whole of life is a predicament, complex and prolonged; and the whole of mind is the cry, prolonged and variously modulated, which that predicament wrings from the psyche.

They express directly her own movements and only indirectly and relatively their external occasion.

After the spirit is born, and in the midst of business has begun to take note silently of the actual aspects and essences of things, the psyche may extend her action with more circumspection, in what we call the arts. That pause, as we may think it, for wonder and contemplation, was only, from her housewife's point of view, a pause for breath: in stopping to gaze, she gives herself time to readjust her impulses and increase her range. Having, among other organs, formed the human hand, she may proceed through that instrument to transform matter outside her body; so that artificial instruments and works become, as it were, organs of the psyche too. With this extension of her instruments her spirit, which is the fruition of them in act, also extends its basis.

Psychic origin and control of the arts.

From her centre, where the spirit lives, she may now control and watch a whole political, industrial, and learned world. Civilisation may accumulate for her benefit a great fund of traditions, which will foster the spirit systematically and direct it rationally. Just as in the growth of the embryo there was a marvellous precision and timeliness in the production of the various organs hereditary in the species, so in animal society there is a great, though much looser, predetermination of what the arts shall produce.

Art, as I use the word here, implies moral benefit: the impulsive modification of matter by man to his own confusion and injury I should not call *The psyche* art, but vice or folly. The tropes of art *and all her* must be concentric with those of health in *works are subject to* the psyche, otherwise they would not, on the *disease.* whole, extend her dominion or subserve her need of discharging her powers. Nature is everywhere full of vices, partly apathetic, in that the impulse at work does not avail to transmute new matter into its instrument, and partly aberrant, in that the impulse itself runs wild, and destroys, instead of buttressing, its original organ—for without an organ an impulse can neither exist nor operate. Thus the psyche continually creates diseases in her substance, or invents scourges and trammels to oppress her from without, as does a false civilisation, through the mad work of her own hands. These aberrations, if extreme, soon defeat themselves by the ruin which they cause; but often they interweave themselves permanently into the strong woof of life, rendering life wretched but not impossible.

In the very inertia of habit, however, as in inveterate vices, there may be a certain luxury or compensation. Impulse, having taken to that trope, may find a certain pleasure in repeating it, a sort of dogged allegiance and sense of rightness, more intimately native and satisfying than any overt proof of its folly. The virtuous human

M

soul, so to speak, is then long dead and buried, and the omnivorous vice has become a soul in its stead. We are compacted of devils. Love and conscience, like the rest, are initially irrational; and the conservative inner man may strenuously cling to methods in art and to forms of sentiment which defeat his eventual rational nature. The fatal imperative of his daemon may lie deeper in him than any ulterior claim of beauty or happiness.

Thus the spiritual function of the psyche is added to her generative and practical functions, creating a fresh and unprecedented realm of being, the realm of spirit, with its original æsthetic spectrum and moral range and values incommensurable with anything but themselves. Yet this whole evocation is a concomitant function of the same psyche which presides over bodily growth and action. Were it not so, spirit would have no place in time or in nature, no relevance to existence, and indeed, no existence of its own; and even if by a flight of mythological fancy we imagined it existing disembodied, it would thereby have forfeited all its dramatic breathlessness, all its moral aspiration, all its piety and potential wisdom. It would be an abstract intellect without a spiritual life, a hypostasis of the realm of truth or of essence, and not a human virtue. So that the dependence of spirit on animal life is no brutal accident, no inexplicable degradation of a celestial being into the soul of a beast. All the themes and passions of spirit, however spiritual or immaterial in themselves, celebrate the vicissitudes of a natural psyche, like a pure poet celebrating the adventures of lovers and kings.

Meantime she has given birth to spirit and attached it to earthly interests.

CHAPTER IX

PSYCHOLOGISM

IF the movements of matter are due to the nature of matter, not to that of spirit, should not the movements of spirit likewise be due to the nature of spirit, not to that of matter? It might seem so: and a great part of human philosophy has been devoted to exploring this tempting path. Yet the issue has been complete confusion; because the nature of spirit is not, like that of matter, to be a principle of existence and movement, but on the contrary a principle of enjoyment, contemplation, description, and belief; so that while spirit manifests its own nature no less freely than matter does, it does so by freely regarding and commenting on something else, either matter or essence: its primary nature is to be secondary —to be observant and intelligent. As grammar is arbiter of the syntax of speech, yet contains no power to determine when anyone shall speak or what he shall wish to say, so spirit contains no principle to determine its own occasions, its distribution in time and place, or the facts that shall seem to confront it. It cannot originate the animal powers and passions which it comes to express. Existence and movement, even in spirit, are therefore the work of matter; while the perception, the enjoyment, the understanding of both matter and spirit are the life of spirit itself. If we

Misguided attempts to represent spirit as master of its own existence and occasions.

163

deny this, and insist on assigning to spirit the functions proper to matter, *spirit, before we know it, has become but another name for matter in our philosophy and in our lives.* In this chapter and in the next I will endeavour to justify this assertion.

That a material force, or all material forces, should be called spirit would be nothing new in the history of language, but rather a reversion to the primitive meaning of the word. Wind is invisible but mighty, and it combines a potentiality of causing total ruin with a gentler habit of filling our sails and doing our work for us. Spirit, a synonym for such a wind, might well be the principle of all action and of all motion. So conceived, it would be precisely that sustaining substance and connecting medium which is requisite to produce feelings consecutively and responsively to one another. It would be what I call the psyche, a reservoir and fountain for the redistribution of energy in the material world, a centre of bodily organisation and action, and simultaneously an organ of sensation, passion, and thought. When people feel a power of origination and decision within them, so that, unless externally hindered, they are free to do whatever they will, undoubtedly they are not deceived. It is not the transforming power of the human heart and brain that any historian of earthly revolutions would be tempted to deny. Human energies have polished the earth's surface and pullulate in it: and it is only too easy for random impulses and contagious phrases to carry mankind away, like sheep after a bellwether. But this guiding or organising or explosive force in animal life is not spirit in any spiritual sense. It is an obscure, complex, groping movement of the psyche, or of many psyches in contact: it is a perpetual readjustment of passionate habits in matter.

Spirit was a name for material force before it was a name for intuition.

When Descartes said that the essence of the soul was to think he gave an excellent definition of spirit; but he initiated a tendency which has dominated modern psychology to its radical disadvantage, the tendency to describe the mind apart from the body and to make psychology merely literary. In his own system the psyche or principle of bodily life was physical and mechanical, and of this true psyche consciousness or thought could only be a concomitant manifestation, and by no means the essence or substance. Nevertheless it was precisely this collateral or ulterior manifestation of the psyche, this conscious spirit, that (because it was the actuality and light of knowledge) became for him and for his followers the one sure existence, and the fulcrum of philosophy: so that since his day philo- But taken sophers have tended to assert that of existence as the we have but this single known or conceivable seat of knowledge, instance—our own feeling or consciousness. spirit may When the relativity of all things to the know- seem to absorb the ledge of them is emphasised, this principle universe. becomes transcendental idealism; but when only the mental nature of all existence, perhaps scattered in many moments and centres, is insisted on, the result is a system of psychological physics which, for convenience, may be called psychologism. This system professes to describe the stuff and constitution of the universe; but it differs from ordinary physics in admitting into its world no elements other than moments of actual experience, as autobiography or dramatic sympathy might catch and describe them. These moments, each only too real in itself, will compose all reality, with nothing latent beneath them, and nothing save other conscious moments possible beyond.

Such a system, though easily conceivable in the abstract, never occurred to the ancients, and would probably never occur to any pure naturalist. Its origin is rather political and poetical: it is humanism become at once radical and sentimental. It sprang up, together with Protestantism and liberalism, out of a worthy but exclusive interest in the inner man. It marks the self-sufficiency of the adult moral individual, forgetful of his origins, and of the external forces which sustain his being. Such reforms often end by abandoning the principle which they seemed at first to exalt, and psychologism in particular may end by denying the existence of consciousness. To one who has never distrusted the orthodox traditions of the human intellect, this conclusion may seem gratuitous and absurd: but it is justified relatively, in compensation for the error of psychologism in making mind absolute, and in pursuance of its critical method: for after all consciousness is directed upon its objects, and knows them before it knows itself.

Psychologism grows out of humanism, which it attempts to make absolute.

The impulse to reduce science to literature was native to humanism and to the whole Renaissance. How much more interesting than logic or theology was the limitless experience which literature could transcribe or suggest! Yet in life a system of science is always involved; and the system assumed by humanists is probably naturalism, which if pressed is materialism; but this is assumed, as all men assume it in daily life, without stopping to defend or to criticise it. To do either would be to become the victim of one of those precarious pedantic dogmatisms which the buxom humanist despises. He lives by a loose naturalism or by a loose religious convention, without examining the principle on which he is living. Nevertheless he is quite positive about the history of the human race, and the variety of its languages, customs, and opinions, including all those conflicting philosophies and religions which, if taken seriously, would prove so inhuman. He may even discourse freely about the

Yet humanism presupposes belief in nature.

causes of events, indulging in prophecy, and leaning towards the higher superstitions, such as the belief in inevitable progress or in laws of history. These prophecies and superstitions, however, can hardly be more than dim perspectives which he thinks he descries in the natural world. History cannot do without geography and material documents and monuments; psychology cannot do without the words and actions of material persons. The humanist inevitably assumes nature reliably at work within and around mankind: a fact which need not prevent him, as it does not prevent the avowed materialist, from relegating the physical world to the background of his thoughts and letting these play by preference on moral and lyrical episodes.

Suppose, however, that we turn this superficial humanism into a dogmatic philosophy and assert that the literary and moral sphere is absolute, so that human experience has always gone on in a vacuum, without any causes, occasions, or existing objects, other than these same successive experiences of particular minds. Would such an all-embracing psychologism compose an adequate system of the universe? For the purposes of the dramatic historian or religious moralist, I think it would. The lives of individuals, as each appears to his own memories and hopes, make up a sort of universal Plutarch, a sufficient handbook for the cure of souls, in which material circumstances need not figure except as picturesque details or landscapes diversifying the experience of those several minds. In sentimental retrospect a man may easily view the scenes of his childhood as having been unsubstantial, and merely a visionary stage-setting to the drama of his young soul. Extending this method to the present and future, we may regard the whole world of history, science, and religion, as internal to the desultory

It may retreat into a personal idealism or monadology.

thoughts in which it is conceived. What a simplifica-
tion of philosophy, what a lightening of the burden of
conventional beliefs! At one stroke the spirit seems
to be liberated from all but spiritual preoccupations,
and all things are reduced to so many pleasing or
oppressive sensations, so many friends or enemies
of our internal liberty and peace.

Such were the systems of Berkeley and Leibniz,
which though very unequal in their technical elaboration, had this radical merit in common: that
they were perfectly lucid and frank about the
ideal or visionary nature of all the possible
data of experience. These data were all
necessarily " inert ideas " or qualities of
feeling; they were essences which did not
and could not exist on their own account. While
they were given they qualified the spirit that contemplated or endured them, and they might then
be said to exist " in the mind "; but it was the perception of them that alone really existed; they were
incapable of subsisting or generating one another in
their own specious or objective plane; they arose and
vanished *in toto*, as did the whole phenomenal world,
with every movement of attention. Thus all images
and terms of thought were impotent and unsubstantial,
yet they were not unmeaning; on the contrary, it was
the very secret of their being that they were signs. In
their variety and movement they composed the language
in which spirit might speak to spirit; and Providence
caused them to arise, as in a prophetic dream, in order
that by their monition and habitual sequence they
might forewarn us and make us ready for their future
harmonies.

These systems were essentially theological; they
invited mankind to substitute a metaphysical faith
in a metaphysical power for the animal faith in matter
by which we are accustomed to live   Verbally the

Berkeley
and Leibniz
recognised
the psychic
ground and
visionary
nature of all
phenomena.

exchange was easy, and might even be emotionally accepted at certain moments of spiritual exaltation, by a person like Malebranche, accustomed to think An ethereal religiously; but the religiosity of Berkeley language and Leibniz was only official; their idealism to express was, and was intended to be, perfectly interests. mundane. Common sense, science, and commerce had no cause to take alarm at it, nor religion to take comfort. In their critical analysis they might sincerely persuade themselves that in looking and touching, in talking and travelling, they were in direct and un-mediated communion with God or with other spirits; but God, at least, was comfortably pledged never to act otherwise than as if matter were acting for him. The muscular idealist could remain wedded in heart and imagination to that material world which he denied in his verbal doctrine. Learning, business, and pro-paganda, tar-water and diplomacy, might occupy him far more absorbingly than any prayerful vision of God, or any suspense of wondering hope on the daily manna of sensation.

Indeed, even in theory, these philosophers were but half-idealists. If they had so easily swept matter away from the landscape of nature—which indeed The soul is a mere image—it was only because, wit- remained tingly or unwittingly, they had packed away a natural all the potency of matter and all its organisa- all its tion into the mysterious mechanism of each and soul, and into the mysterious interaction of relations. one soul with another. Spirit had not only become again a wind, an invisible power, but each spirit separately, or the swarm of spirits collectively, had become a world of unfathomable generative processes—a world far less observable, and no less mechanical, than the earth and sky of vulgar philosophy. These souls without bodies continued to be full of hidden poten-tialities and blind passions; they lasted through a time which being common to them all was not specious and imaginary, but physical and independent of the temporal perspectives within each of them. They were buffeted by collateral contacts or compulsions which virtually subjected them to existence in a physical space. If they did not exert physical force upon one another, at least they interchanged telephonic messages through a sort of central exchange established in the divine mind. Remove matter, thought Berkeley, and you remove all danger of atheism. It did not occur to him to ask in what respect God would differ from matter if the divine function was simply to excite sensation and to supply a medium for psychic telegraphy. He blandly supposed that the alternative to matter was the God of Christianity: but we know that his psychological scepticism, when carried out, will undermine all Christian legend and all Christian cosmology.

A God who was a supreme spirit, like the God of Aristotle and Plotinus, would be immutable: his action on the world could only occur through an eternal attraction or effluence, enabling or soliciting matter to take such forms as matter at each point might be capable of taking. If we wish to avoid this conclusion, and to regard divine action as incidental and occasional, God becomes a natural being, like the gods of legend and mythology, living in time, discovering piecemeal his own preferences, recasting his plans, and parrying the blows of fortune or of free-will in others, like any proud animal, with ever-fresh ingenuity and explosions of temper. Such are the moral powers actually at work in the world; some of them might be superhuman; but in any case they would be internal to the field of action, and would inhabit the material agencies by which they were manifested: so that the belief in interaction and intercommunication between so-called

God, too, became again a material agent.

spirits is really a belief in the realm of matter, and in the interplay there of various living centres.

This conclusion is indeed implicit in the principle by which the realm of matter is posited in the beginning. If spirits are agents, they can be discovered only by being posited in the field of action, and only by virtue of their functions there. Like matter they will be names for the responsive and calculable energies which are there at work. *This follows from the nature and occasion of animal faith.* But that which fills the field of action, and is unequally distributed there, being nearer or farther, mightier or weaker, in discoverable measures; that which is in perpetual motion, compelling us to act in time by its definite pressure or allurements; that which acts within us mysteriously in response, and which preserves the effects of our action in the form of readiness and habit—this, by definition, is matter itself: and this definition, I think, is by no means arbitrary, but scrupulously faithful to the normal force of the word, and to its spontaneous application. Therefore the spirits posited by Berkeley, Malebranche, and Leibniz, or by anyone who thinks of spirits as powers, are simply mythological names for certain operations of matter, poetically apprehended, and turned into dramatic units with reference to the observer's interests or emotions. Human spirits are such mythological units corresponding to the actions or surviving effects of human bodies; and God is such a mythological name for the universal power and operation of matter.

Indeed, the more critical advocates of psychologism have abandoned, at least in theory, all notion of spirits, powers, or agents; and for them the universe is composed exclusively of momentary feelings, for whose existence, number, quality, or order no reason at all can be given or required. It *If feelings have no ground, how have they an order?* is perhaps not very clear to a materialist how sensations arise in bodies; but is it clearer to the pure psychologist how they should arise in nothing and out of nothing? It is true that existence is contingent in any case and ultimately groundless; but in psychologism this initial marvel is continually recurrent. Sensations and ideas are supposed to be many: each pops of itself into existence; yet nothing—since nothing else exists—can possibly condition their genesis or subtend their variety. Each, no less than the order of all, is absolutely uncaused and might just as well have been entirely different. Nevertheless the advocate of psychologism seems never to doubt that they all spring up as seasonably as the leaves of a tree; they seem to be miraculously revealed to him, who is at any moment only one of them, in their variegated character and precise distribution. Something, which he says is nothing, compels each to bide its own time and makes it cognisant of the existence and order of the rest.

This assumption of inexplicable transcendent knowledge is so lightly made because psychologism is not an original or primary conviction, but a critical reform introduced into a conventional naturalism. Its categories are secondary naturalistic categories—those of history and social imagination—and they are employed unchallenged after the primary categories—those of action and practical art—have been theoretically abandoned. But this reliance on the secondary is fallacious and must be short-lived. Spirits and laws, for a natural philosopher, are simply names bestowed humanly on the habits of bodies. Remove the bodies, and the spirits and laws have lost their sole natural status and means of manifestation. Nevertheless the literary psychologist may still live on for a while, like the ruminating camel in the desert, on the momentum of his unconsumed moral provisions; and he may imagine spirits and laws to retain their office in respect of his private experience, after they have lost their meaning and application in nature.

Moral society is an overture of material relations.

He may deny the natural world, and yet suppose himself living in a natural society.

That psychologism leans throughout on a tacit materialism appears clearly in the only principle which, so far as I know, it has ever invoked to describe the course of immediate experience— I mean the principle of association of ideas. This principle is clearly secondary: at best it is a principle of revival, occasionally exemplified in memory and reverie. Even supposing (what is manifestly false) that we always reviewed events in the order in which they first occurred, how should this law explain the order in which they arose originally? Yet the original order of events is the very subject of natural philosophy—the one thing which science and practical art are concerned to discover and to understand; and of this order association affords no explanation. If psychologism were not implicitly materialistic, it would be a proclamation of complete isolation and helplessness in the midst of a presumable chaos. Each man at each moment would tremblingly be the sensation he was: and if that sensation placed him in the presence of any imagined story or any fantastic world, nothing whatever would indicate that this groundless experience of to-day would have any sequel to-morrow. This is actually the attitude of moral anarchists, such as some of the heroes of modern fiction and some of the authors, who seem actually to take seriously the romantic conceit that experience is something absolute. But sanity assumes the opposite; and the prosperous arts which are the fruit of sanity prove that experience is a perpetually evanescent and most sensitive index to an order of nature beneath it.

> How, in the absence of animal bodies, shall experience be initiated or controlled?

Let us still suppose, however, that the universe might be simply a multitude of islets of feeling, each existing for itself. Each would then be distinguished from the rest only by its felt quality or (what is the same thing) by the quality and complexity of the essence revealed in it.   There would be a sort of nebula of states of mind; and we should have to ask ourselves in what sense, and in what medium, if in any, they could be said to be successive or in any way earlier or later than one another.   I have observed above [1] that when succession is actually enacted and is not merely specious or intuited, it is an external relation: the first state is lost in attaining the second.   Now if these states were feelings distinguished only by their essences, they would stand in purely internal and eternal relations to one another; they could not be successive; there would be no possible transition from the one into the other, since there would be neither a flow of substance nor a leaping thought to effect the passage.   I need not dwell on the corollary that in that case they could not even exist, but would have receded into their respective essences, and would radically fail to compose the elements or moments of a changing world.   Let me admit for the sake of argument that they might exist by virtue of some stress or oscillation internal to each of them: what meaning could there then be in saying that they were successive or existed at different dates?   Within each there would be no conceivable evidence of a time when it was not or of a time when it no longer should be.   If they are events, as in psychologism they are taken to be, *they must transform something pre-existent, which they at once replace and continue*.   They must be portions of a longer event, incidents in an existential field protracted beyond any one of them.   Is it not evident that we are positing a physical time beneath and beyond them in which they may be dated and distributed?   But I have previously found that physical time cannot be divorced from physical space, nor either of them from the flux of

How can absolute sensations be successive?

_____

[1] See pp. 11 and 80.

matter; and this conclusion will impose itself on the critical psychologist quite apart from any mathematical or astronomical arguments which may also support it. For the psychologist differs from the pure logician or poet in that he assumes memory to be constitutionally veracious and self-transcendent, reporting a series of past or outlying events which have been and are materially separate: he is a naturalist and a realist in method. His world has a single history, and involves lateral contacts and forward transmissions which are external to the natural moments concerned. One natural moment is, even for him, *materially* the heir to another and *physically* the neighbour to a third or a fourth. Psychological facts, if they are to be temporal and connected events, are therefore inconceivable except in the realm of matter.

Perhaps a critic inclined to a transcendental view of mind might here take the bull by the horns and might urge that of course psychological facts are not temporal events at all, and that indeed they have only internal relations to one another. What affinity should spiritual existence have to a pervasive and endless flux, when the very nature of spirit is to be synthetic, and in each of its instances an absolute centre of survey and of judgment? How should actual intuitions impinge upon a physical time or be scattered over it like daisies in a field or pins in a pin-cushion? This is an alien relation imputed to spiritual facts by the materialising imagination, which attaches them to bodies and events in a conventional world. In themselves, acts of cognition may picture time but cannot sprawl over it; yet the pictured time in them amply suffices to link them ideally together into phases of a common ideal drama. Like the episodes in a novel or the series of whole numbers, without having any fixed physical date, they may

Suggestion that the essential relations of spiritual moments might suffice to render them ideally successive.

compose an order of logical succession by virtue of their deliverance, if one contains, so to speak, a front view and another a rear view of the same imaginary objects. What to one living moment is a hope, to another living moment is a memory; and these complementary perspectives place them vicariously in one specious time, like the earlier and the later speeches in the same play, without any actual or physical derivation of one cognitive moment from another.

Who would not gladly dwell on these intrinsic contrasts and harmonies in the moral spectrum, by which all possible states of the spirit are diversified? But I am not here concerned with establishing any spiritual hierarchy or setting up any Jacob's ladder; I am concerned only with the current assumption that feelings and ideas having no material basis may yet have a temporal order. And is it not obvious that if we truly limited our view to the mental sphere, it would be gratuitous ever to posit anything not given? But that which is given at any moment or in any experience is necessarily internal to it. In pure intuition all perspectives contain and exhaust their entire objects; time and space are there specious only. The only thinkable or discoverable sequence touching such states of mind is the sense of succession perhaps given in some of them: a succession which does not connect these states with one another, but only the specious elements, within each, between which it feels a transition. History will all be contained in mirrors, themselves existing in no temporal medium. Each moment of experience will be a monad without windows, but with variously painted walls. It will have no date and no surroundings; like a room in a historical museum it will bear the name and suggest the atmosphere of some age and country otherwise unknowable to us, and now non-existent; but for the sincere idealist, who posits no

Moral relations cannot constitute a physical order.

truth beyond his living intuition, this represented
existence will seem quite satisfying. Without ever
needing to quit his museum, he can survey the panorama of all these historic essences in their fabulous
progression; the same history being surveyed at each
point from a different angle, and knitting all admissible
vistas together into one moral world.

We are at the threshold of transcendental idealism:
to pass through we need only add this reflection: as
all given times or spaces must be imaginary
and internal to the act of intuition which First way out from
surveys them, so the assumed multiplicity psycho-
of these acts must be itself imaginary and logism: into transcend-
internal to the idea or sense of their multi- ental idealism.
plicity. Self-consciousness will then have
truly swallowed up all its objects, and we shall have
passed out of psychologism by the subjective door.
We shall have retained and made absolute the activity
of spirit: and by force of this initial assurance we shall
have destroyed the presuppositions and the problem
of psychologism; for we shall no longer posit a naturalistic flux of feelings and ideas, running down somehow
in a common time, and somehow divided into separate
series called individual lives. Those imagined feelings
and ideas, with the conventional divisions and connections established among them, will be reduced to
elements in a picture painted by the spirit in the
idealist, and existing only under the unity of his
apperception, in which they are obviously interrelated
and inseparable. The specious world so conceived, we
shall see presently, remains material; but the philosopher
has become a genuine idealist, because (except when he
forgets himself) he attributes no existence to that world
apart from his conception.

But psychologism, though inwardly condemned to
die, is free to choose among various forms of suicide.
Instead of perishing by concentration in the ego, it

N

may perish by diffusion among images, tropes, and phenomena. The ingredients of the universe will still

Second way out: into pheno-menalism or pictorial physics.

be sought in feelings and acts of intuition which are spiritual events and subjective. Yet the philosopher will not banish from his mind the common assumption that nature exists in her own right and is a perfectly well-known congeries of material objects and events. The consequence is that when he becomes a psychological critic of experience, and endeavours to reform and reconstruct his picture of reality exclusively out of his immediate data, he continues in possession, *de facto* though not *de jure*, of the conventional lines of nature on which to hang the family linen of his mind. Feelings and acts of intuition make manifest certain essences which, although intrinsically only logical, æsthetic, or moral universals, are often impulsively taken for parts of the objects which evoke them; or in other cases, when feelings have only obscure physiological causes, the moral essences given in these feelings are regarded as parts of the body which feels them. Thus a landscape is taken by the innocent tourist to be the intrinsic essence of the region he traverses; and a pain passes mythically for an existing force within the aching part, causing its contraction and all its ensuing acts. When this propensity is dominant in the philosopher, and at the same time he is jealous of the certitude of immediate experience, he is likely to abandon his psychologism by the objective door. He will overlook as far as possible the spiritual centre of his experience and the organic seat and significance of his perceptions, and he will construct out of his given essences, like a poet, a many-coloured garment for nature. His psychologism will become a sort of sensuous realism or pictorial metaphysics. The materials will be ideal, the events subjective, but they will be deployed in a posited time and space, and supplemented hypothetically by imaginary phenomena, so as to compose a panoramic world—a continuum of ephemeral images and impulses having a certain material breadth and interconnection.

Theories of this sort might seem, in one direction, more materialistic than materialism, since they ignore or deny the existence of spirit; but perhaps the omission is more apparent than real. In the lottery of opinion, when schools are bewildered and categories are in solution, spirit may be eliminated in the ostensible result only because it was secretly presupposed in the inquiry. Phenomenalism, logicism, and pictorial realism all start from personal experience and are abstractions from it; they analyse the objects engaging a living spirit which prefers to forget itself, with its perpetually central station and dogmatic energy. What is a phenomenon? Is it an essence given in intuition? Certainly that is what any phenomenon becomes to a radical critic. Or is it a fact posited by an assertive and aggressive mind that regards given essences as substantive existences in their own specious plane? That is what a phenomenon seems to be to animal illusion and dramatic fancy. But the truth is that immediate feeling, whether excited by the eye or by some inner organ, is most thoroughly a product of the living psyche, and expresses her animal passions: how then should the qualities felt in these feelings be detached from the psyche, in which alone they can arise or live? How should they subsist, dead, dried, and insensible, in the external cosmic order of the objects posited and encountered in action?

Nature reduced to a description of nature in visual and mathematical terms.

Nor is it only the trembling visions visiting the soul that suffer and die in that transposition; the dynamic objects for which they are substituted suffer an equal injury. For these are now emptied of their active unfathomable substance, which renders them co-ordinate

with the active self in our own bodies; they are reduced to films and conceived surfaces, if not to mere
Shadowy   words or mathematical equations. These thin
character of sensuous or intelligible essences are then
pheno-
menalistic multiplied and hypothetically interpolated *ad*
science.   *libitum*, in order to fill the enormous spaces
and the abysses of time which actual experience must
leave unexplored in any world supposed to be continuous
and self-subsisting. Recent science has been very inventive in this direction, and technically profound in
proportion to the intellectual initiative displayed in it;
but, after all, the truth of all these images and tropes,
or even their applicability to nature, depends on their
just contacts, first, with the conventional field of action,
and secondly, with the experience of the questioning
soul.

A philosopher who would place all this literary
psychology and optical physics where they belong,
All object- needs to stand firm in his native centre. He
ive idealisms is a spirit, and his life is a dream; but this
are funda-
mentally   dream when trusted and pressed, as it must
subjective. be in action, involves the mysterious fecundity
of a psyche which may breed this sustained dream in
its vegetative and passionate order; and this psyche
in turn involves a material world in which she may
weave her organism and try her fortunes. Her
fecundity as well as her adventures must be initially
blind, since they create in her the first glimmer of
ideas; and they must be mechanical, if they are supposed to depend on the interaction of various psyches,
or various organic impulses, in some medium in which
they have arisen and continue to reside. Above all,
this cosmic flux is nothing phenomenal, nor composed
of visual images or tropes and mathematical laws: it
is in itself what it is, and for us what it does. Our
sensuous and conceptual experience touches but does
not lift the hem of that garment from which its virtue

flows. Phenomena are all like the rainbow, products of a point of view. Permanent or surely recurrent as they may sometimes be, they are so only from a particular station; they vanish on a nearer approach, and change their essence at a different angle. Uprooted from the organ and occasion that support them, they vanish like ghosts without leaving even a bone or a shroud behind. It is only in memory or fancy that any vestige of phenomena remains; only legend can record their order. And these evanescent views have no seat in nature, except perhaps—indirectly and unobservably—in some labouring brain. Traced home, they are moments in some biography, revelations within some personal experience. They lead us back, therefore, to a monadism or solipsism, in which the philosopher finds himself in the presence of nothing but a dream of which he can discern neither the extent nor the meaning. Phenomenalism and its kindred systems may indeed abolish the spirit from their objective cosmos, because this cosmos is itself initially and ultimately visionary, and exists only for the spirit that conceives it.

There are advocates of psychologism to whom the vanity of this conclusion is obvious and who revert from it to the substantial part of their world, namely, to the self or psyche, since it is only there that any phenomenal system can touch actual existence. Yet for them the psyche *Third way out: into panpsychism.* can be composed only of moments of consciousness; feelings and intuitions form her whole substance; and if reality is to lie anywhere deeper than the level of conventional ideas or to explain their origin and composition, it will be necessary very much to extend the field of literary psychology, and to supply no end of unknown feelings and ideas between and beyond those posited by common opinion. Evidence is not wanting to convince us that many such feelings and ideas exist,

either buried and ignored in ourselves, or proper to
the different quality of other living spirits. Human
fancy, if inclined sometimes to invent spirits that do
not exist, is also constitutionally incapable of conceiving and crediting the experience of any existing spirits
too remote from itself. Nature is in every way richer
than our thoughts of nature, and the hypothesis deserves respect that many a form of experience exists,
within us and beyond, which our conventional human
thoughts cannot appreciate. Such unremembered,
dispersed, or alien sensibility is often called unconscious mind—a relative and egotistical name for it,
since if alien feelings are unconscious to us,
our feelings are no less unconscious to them.
Yet perhaps, under this unjust designation,
there may lurk a secret reversion to pheno-
menalism. " Unconscious mind " may suggest an essence or a series of essences which,
under other circumstances, would be manifest to a
mind generated by those circumstances: and these
essences may be conceived as existing somehow without any intuition of them, as if they could be formed
and dissolved in the dark, by a sort of nebular evolution.
But the given or phenomenal is relative to spirit; it
cannot arise if not synthesised in an act of intuition;
and it cannot be preserved or revived in the unconscious, or set out in a physical time and space to compose a crepuscular mental cosmos, partly illuminated
and partly darkened, like the moon. The bright part
only will be the field of mind, the rest will be the field
of matter; and the field of mind will not be substantially independent or of fixed extent, but will describe
so much of the field of matter as the light of intuition
or understanding has chanced to play upon. If those
unconsidered sensations or wishes are mental at all,
they must shine each for itself, even if invisible to one
another. A pain or a sound is either felt and heard,

Marginal note: Unconscious mind a name for conscious mind elsewhere or for what is not mind at all.

or it recedes into the structure, tension, and rhythms of the material world; and only the latter can be designated by the term " unconscious ", if this term be taken absolutely and not relatively. An appeal to the unconscious would then mark the surrender of psychologism.

If we disdain this surrender, and insist on conceiving a universe made up of mental events, may we not posit a compact flux of feelings, such as our waking and dreaming life seems actually to be, only more voluminous, consequential, and complex, so that the interstices of our remembered experience shall be filled in with continuous forgotten feelings and thoughts? And similarly, might not the interstices between the experiences of various selves be filled in with some sort of inner animation, constituting the substance of the world everywhere, even in all the apparently empty stretches of space and time, when these stretches really exist or lapse? This would imply psychic mortar no less than psychic stones. Not only would all reality be a flux of feelings and imagery, as in a dream, but all dreams, divide them as we may into dramatic episodes and private lives, would be continuous and mutually derivative, so that no dream would ever begin save by continuing or uniting previous dreams, nor end save in the act of generating new ones.

Panpsychism a conceivable hypothesis.

This seems to be a logical possibility. Panpsychism is free from that covert reliance on matter by which all other idealisms subsist, and it seems less superficial. Its universe is composed of states of mind generating and emptying into one another; so that while its substance is feeling, to the satisfaction of our pensive self-consciousness and moral pride, this feeling is distributed and condensed just as matter would be in a material world. Therefore while panpsychism seems to cover the whole realm of matter and so to render other matter superfluous, the question is how far it differs from materialism in its texture. Is it anything but materialism strained through a psychological sieve?

The use of psychological or even mythological language—as is done in psycho-analysis—would not be of great consequence, if physical facts and relations were always signified: but the axiom of panpsychism is that all facts are mental, and the question arises: How can mental facts compose a natural world? If the relations between them are mental, they are not natural; and if they are natural they are not mental.

But in multiplying mental states ad infinitum it leaves them without connections.

There is, for instance, a felt continuity in mental life, of which many a moment is conscious, but this felt continuity within given perspectives is not an actual continuity between successive events. The first moment of life begins without consciousness of beginning, and the last moment ends without possible consciousness of having ended. If in any experience the first moment were also the last—as in some sense is always the case, since each moment has a self-existent life which cannot be stretched—this isolated moment of consciousness would not be aware of its punctiform station in the world of events, but would look before and after, and blankly about, as if it had cognitive dominion and large participation in the material universe to which its organ belongs. It has such participation spiritually, being spiritual itself: but the dramatic vista within it cannot enable it to pass physically out of itself into the next actual feeling. Those features in its internal revelation between which a felt continuity obtains are given essences, here forming a perspective in which moments are not self-existent, but imperfectly realised by virtue of felt contrasts, and therefore inseparable. Even if the terms, half-distinguished in this uncertain continuum, were descriptive of ulterior events, the vision of them (with its degree of the partiality and redundance proper to mental reactions) would be a fresh event on its own account. It would be as helpless as any other immaterial fact to flow into other facts, or to lie among them in a physical time and space.

On the other hand, the existence of continuity in events, were there no material psyche to synthesise and collect their successiveness in her enriched powers, could not yield a sense of continuity, or any other sort of knowledge. Merely being a fact can never cause a fact to be discovered. An organ of sense must first become sensitive to that fact and must impose some subjective view of it on intuition. In a world of mental events all the connections of these events must still remain physical: they cannot be numbered among those events. It is therefore not true, even on this view, that the world is composed of mental events exclusively; they are assumed to impinge on a deeper medium in which they arise, and which supplies all their existential relations.

Perhaps without altogether dismissing these considerations, it might be urged that there is one spiritual reality, the Will, which supplies precisely the transitive bond required between living moments. What is this Will? All that a literary psychologist can consistently understand by the word is the *sense* of willing— the feeling of glad action, the preferences, expectations, wishes, purposes, and decisions which may traverse his mind. Did he conceive the Will to be a transitive power, by which ulterior states of mind were positively created or transformed, he would be appealing to something physical or divine beyond consciousness, something of which the wishes or decisions occurring in consciousness would be only omens or symptoms. Energetic idealists are victims of an illusion: the more they insist on Will, Life, Vital Impulse, or the Eternal

Will is either a mental phenomenon like any other, and impotent, or else a physical or divine power beyond the range of psychologism.

Feminine, the more decidedly they turn away from synthetic mind and lay up their treasures in the flux of matter. What else is that mounting energy which they feel within themselves and in all nature, and which they justly recognise as far deeper and more pervasive than any images or conceptions of the reasoning mind? An immense and intricate flow of substance has formed their organisms, and thereby determined their purposes and passions: for evidently purposes, wishes, and preferences are just as secondary, just as much synthetic and expressive, as are the data of sense, and all images and memories. All these are bred in animal organs and presuppose a prior direction of unconscious life.

Panpsychism accordingly involves and posits the realm of matter: for it disposes the elements known to literary psychology in a cosmic system which they can neither compose nor support. The panpsychist merely maintains—what in some sense may be quite true—that the realm of matter is throughout animate; and he chooses to regard this animation, in deference to his humanistic and literary habit of mind, as substantial, ignoring the far deeper fatality, which he can hardly deny, by which all this animation is distributed: a fatality which when recognised, posited, and studied, alone justifies any mind in imagining and addressing certain other minds, or its own natural destinies.

Panpsychism is materialism translated into psychological terms.

There is a final or vanishing form of panpsychism in which this implication is virtually admitted, and the universe is said to be composed of mind-stuff, or matter of such a sort that mind may arise out of it. This is a radically different theory from the panpsychism considered above, in which minds or sensations, conscious though perhaps feeble and vague, were made the stuff of the universe. That true matter is of such a sort that mind may arise

When the elements of the psychic universe are admitted to be unconscious, the distinction from materialism becomes merely verbal.

out of it every materialist must allow; the question
is only what conception of matter this circumstance
compels or permits us to form. Shall we think of it
as dust quickened, or as life dissipated, extinguished,
and reduced to atoms?

To assert that the substance of anything, much less
of the whole world, was psychic, and to call it mind-
stuff, would be inadmissible if we meant that
minute but conscious spirits were the stuff of it:
we have just seen the manifold impossibility of
that. But the phrase becomes legitimate and
significant if it serves only to remind us that
physical, like spiritual, existence must be intensive,
centred in each of its parts, and capable of inner change
as well as of collateral reduplication. We should never
broach existence at all if we cut up phenomena into
minima sensibilia, or traversed the intellectual landscape
in a thousand ways in order to establish, by intense
intuition of its essence, all sorts of contrasts and
relations between its specious elements. Intellectual
landscapes vary with intelligence, not to say with
fashion; and *minima sensibilia* vary with the faculties
of sense. The actual reality in a man is himself, not
his imagined objects: and it is on the level of his active
being, and on the analogy of his progressive and self-
annihilating existence, that other existences are to be
conceived.

> Physical existence is more analogous to mind than to ideas.

The substance of nature, thus diffused and, in spots,
concentrated into organisms, becomes in these organisms also the substance of mind. It must evidently
have been perfectly fitted to produce everything which
it actually produces; it may therefore be decorated
retrospectively, by a Chinese piety, with all the titles
won by its children; indeed, these its eventual manifestations are the sole index which we possess to its
intrinsic nature.

Now the fact that substance can sometimes live and

think shows that any pictorial or mathematical description of it cannot be exhaustive or even intensively very penetrating; such descriptions mark rather the external order proper to substance in its diffusion and interaction, and supply a notation suitable for mapping it or building in it. At the same time that which thinks in an animal is unmistakably the same substance as that which lives and moves in him: his mind shares the fortunes of his body and exists only by realising its contacts and its interests. Therefore while the designation of substance as mind-stuff is correct, it is by no means exclusively, or even pre-eminently proper. Even in animals, not to speak of nature in general, the inclination of existence towards thought is neither radical nor general; and the substance of this world is far more fundamentally designed for sleeping than for waking. In so far as mind has stuff at all under it and is not purely spiritual, the stuff of it is ordinary matter. We can observe and trace the organic bodies which naturally possess feeling, or cause spirit to awake within them; but who shall observe or imagine an organic concourse of unconscious atoms of mind? Moreover, organisation requires a medium as well as a stuff; and the medium in which mind-stuff moves is avowedly physical space and time. But what can exist in space except matter, and what except matter can be the vehicle of true derivation and continuity in a truly lapsing time? Mind-stuff is therefore simply an indirect name for matter, given in deference to an idealistic bias surviving the wreck of idealism; and nothing but a confusing attachment to a psychological vocabulary could counsel its frequent use.

I find, then, that in the psychological sphere, apart from pure feeling or intuition, everything is physical. There is no such thing as mental substance, mental

[Marginal note:] Though matter may be called mind-stuff, that designation is marginal and not central.

force, mental machinery, or mental causation. If actual feelings or intuitions have any ground at all this ground is physical; if they have a date, place, or occasion they have it only in the physical world. Physical, too, is the determination of their quality and diversity, of their meaning or intent, of their affinities and development; physical their separation into particular lives as well as their union, in each person, into a particular sequence or strand of experiences. Physical, finally, is the sole evidence open to any mind of the existence or character of minds in others. Psychology, therefore, when it does more than evoke poetically various dramatic feelings or intuitions, traces the behaviour of living bodies—which includes their language—interpreting it in moral terms; and it cannot compose a system of the universe out of these moral terms abstracted from their physical backing, because this backing alone supplies their existential connections and historical order. Thus psychology reports certain complications in the realm of matter: and the interpretations which may be added in terms of spirit depend entirely for their truth on the existence and spiritual fertility of that material background.

CHAPTER X

THE LATENT MATERIALISM OF IDEALISTS

WHAT is idealism? I should like to reply: Thought and love fixed upon essence. If this definition were

Idealism a moral interest dictating a physical system.

accepted idealism would be a leaven rather than a system, because although essence is everywhere present it never occurs alone, but either as the form of some existing thing or event, or else as a term given in intuition; so that however sceptical or contemplative the philosopher might be, his own existence at least would be a fact eluding his idealism and prerequisite to it. He could become a complete idealist only by forgetting himself, and not inquiring into the origin or meaning of his quite contingent existence and quite arbitrary visions. To arrest attention on pure essence and to be an idealist in a moral or poetic sense, would therefore be possible to a man holding any system of physics. Even a materialist might be a true idealist, if he preferred the study of essence to that of matter or events; but his natural philosophy would keep his poetic ecstasies in their proper place. Such an equilibrium, however, has seldom recommended itself to professed philosophers, whose virtue has impelled them rather to push their favourite insights into the absolute, and assert the universe to be the perfect mirror of their minds. Those who have been idealists by temperament have been accordingly inclined to substitute essence for matter in their theory of the universe. Their hearts, had they not done so, would have been painfully divided; for the most fervent and contemplative idealist is still a man and an animal, and nature has initially directed his attention and passion not on essence, but on fact, on power, on the factors of his material destiny. The more impetuous his idealism and the more unitary his dogmatic mind, the greater need he will find of fusing his physics with his visions, and assigning to the system of essences which fills his imagination the position and the powers of matter. Hence a gnostic physics in which chosen ideas pass for facts and felt values for powers: and it is this superstition, and not the pure study and love of essence, that is commonly known as idealism.

The earliest and noblest form of this idealism was the doctrine of the Platonic Socrates. In somewhat playfully defining the current terms of speech, he very earnestly disentangled the types of moral excellence and the goals of political wisdom. His Ideas were fundamentally ideals, forms which things would approximate in proportion as they approached perfection, each after its kind. It was in this measure also that things deserved their names and could be justly subsumed under their class in the hierarchy of objects important to the legislator and having fixed functions in the economy of life. Nothing could have a nature unless it had a possible perfection: that which rendered a bed " really " a bed, or a bridle " really " a bridle was their respective functions; for it was as better fitted to sleep in soundly or to rein in horses effectively that beds and bridles were better or worse, or were beds and bridles at all. Reality and excellence thus coincided and came from participation in some Idea; for this Platonic sort of reality was altogether supernal and had nothing to do with existence. Filth and hair also existed; but unless

Socratic idealism at first purely moral and spiritual.

they found a use and had a consequent standard of perfection—for instance, as fur or as manure—they fell under no Idea, and the rational moralist might ignore them. The wise and prudent man was quick to see the ideal in the material; and he prized existence only for the sake of the ever-bright essence of the good which in a thousand colours and degrees shone darkly through it.

This initial phase of Platonism is pregnant with several different possibilities, all of which, perhaps, have not been noticed or developed. In one direction, for instance, it points to super-naturalism, to the conviction that the soul would never find her true good until she was disembodied and identified in contemplation with the ideas which were her natural food. Only in that heaven would there be happiness, where, as in Nirvana, there would be no change, no division, and in that sense no existence. For if things draw all their virtue from ulterior perfections which they can only embody imperfectly, evidently it would have been simpler and better to have begun at the end, to have always possessed the good in its perfection, and to have been spared the pain and indignity of alienation from it. This view was actually recommended by the Platonic Socrates in his last hours; probably at any other time it would have proved embarrassing, and we need not wonder that it remained in abeyance. Had it been pressed, what would have become of that sane plebeian wisdom of Socrates, austerely reducing all beauty to health, all virtue to circumspect knowledge, and all good to utility for pleasure? Evidently in heaven there would be no place any longer for beds and bridles, for ogling love, or for the restless yearning to bring all things to birth in beauty. Indeed, it is much to be feared that without those humble natural occasions and animal functions demanding to be perfected, per-

All its virtue came from its material foundation.

fection itself and the good would have entirely vanished. Had the divine sufficiency of the Ideas in their own realm been seriously maintained, this supernaturalism, by transcending morality and abolishing preference, would have clearly shown that the foundation of Socratic idealism was material.

Matter is indeed indispensable to any system in which the supreme reality is divine and eternal, because without matter that reality could have no manifestation in space, time, persons, and contingent circumstances. This was acknowledged by the Platonists more frankly *Confusion of physical substance with materia prima.* and intelligently than by modern idealists; yet while admitting this fundamental function of matter, they represented it as wholly negative and passive, the forms which it took being imposed upon it from above, by the divine virtue of Ideas regarded as magnets. This view was protected by two equivocations, on which the whole of Platonising physics depends. One equivocation consisted in substituting the essence of materiality, itself an Idea, for the locally existing and variegated substance of material things. The essence of materiality, being defined by negation of all forms, was pure nonentity; its vacuity could be easily proved to contribute nothing to the positive essence of anything; and the bewildered disciple was expected never to perceive that, even if things owed no part of their form to abstract matter, they owed to their concrete matter the possibility of their existence. For if matter was universal inertia, it was also universal potentiality: and by admitting, as Ideas do not, a contingent selection and flux of forms, it admitted life, motion, and particular existences, and enabled one Idea to manifest itself here and another there in varying degrees of perfection.

The other equivocation, intertwined with this, turned on the double use of the word " make " : for a principle of form " makes " a thing what it is, by justifying its title to a certain name or to a certain estimation; whereas its substance and origin cannot lie there, but must be supplied in the flux of existence by matter predisposed to assume that form, and material agencies at hand, able to impose that possible form upon that special matter. For the material cause of anything is not the essence of materiality, but rather a certain quantity of matter already endowed with form, with local existence, and with internal and surrounding tensions calculated to change its condition. This existing matter in its spontaneous movement is the force at work in the genesis of one thing out of another. Ideas at best can be only the formal or final causes of their exemplification: they are not forces at all, but qualities and harmonies resulting from the concourse of material facts: and to say that the form or function of anything " makes " it what it is, is a mere play on the ambiguity of words and a solemn mystification.

Confusion of formal with efficient cause.

That the Ideas are powerless, and that power is perpetually ascribed to them only by a figure of speech, due to a natural impulse in idealists toward indiscriminate eulogy of whatever is formal and describable, I think may be made evident by a single consideration. Platonic Ideas are eternal. Whatsoever hierarchy they may compose, and whatever radiance may issue from them, magically capable of transmuting matter into their likeness, this effluence is perpetual. All the Ideas are always equally inviting and potent: their generous creative virtue pours forth from them impartially at all seasons, in all directions, and to all distances. In a word, they are not physical facts or physical forces at all, but purely logical essences. They are intrinsically without the least bond or the least relevance to any particular point of time or region of space. What-

Eternal forms cannot be the cause of particular incidents.

ever magic attraction they may be reputed to exercise over matter, they will exercise over it equally everywhere and at all times. On the other hand, the face of nature is diversified, and the facts that here exemplify those essences are unevenly distributed, often repeated, and almost always imperfect reproductions of their ideal originals.

Why, then, is any Idea manifested here and not there, perfectly or imperfectly, once, often, or not at all? I know of but one conceivable answer. *The cause can only be the varied predispositions of matter.* Because of the different predispositions of the diffuse matter concerned. In respect to any particular event, or to the form of any particular thing or action, the cause of occurrence or non-occurrence can only lie in the material situation at the previous moment—the structure and movement of the substance at hand under those material circumstances. We may rhetorically assign all virtue to the Idea then realised, since this is the marvel open to intuition in which alone the spirit is ultimately interested. Yet it was matter that determined whether that virtue should be exercised in any particular case; so that matter alone is responsible for what occurs, although the Ideas which it brings to light may get all the credit of it.

This predisposition in matter illustrates the fundamental contingency of existence, and in that respect may be likened to absolute free will; we might *This is a primal accident like absolute free will, but morally free will presupposes a formed nature.* fancifully say that an absolutely free will in matter was the ground of everything. But such a radical and initial fatality has nothing in it of intelligent freedom, such as appears in actions expressive of the ingrained bent of living creatures, actions adapted to the circumstances, and prophetic of the result which, if fortunate, they are likely to have. Such moral power of self-expression is possible only because that previous fatality, or free will in the sense of absolutely ground-less action, has already established particular psyches and initiated in them an effort towards specific kinds of perfection. At whatever point we call a halt in our backward survey of history, we find extant some arbitrary state of things, determining the forms which intelligent judgment and action shall then assume. A psyche is presupposed distinguishing and declaring good those characters which, were she omnipotent, she would impose on everything: characters which things will hardly acquire in fact, since many forces besides those centred in the psyche will conspire to shape the issue. Thus the initiation, distribution, and transmission of existing forms, when traced to their source, are entirely the work of matter.

If instead of matter we posit a deity or a moral force or a special dialectic to be the first principle of existence, the case is not essentially altered. Any other efficient cause would be equally contingent and, in respect to spirit, equally material. Such a deity or dialectic or moral force would then be the primal accident, the groundless fact, the one form of being which existence happened to wear in neglect of all other forms; and that which distinguishes matter from essence—its exclusive potentialities—would distinguish that supposed metaphysical agency just as truly, and just as arbitrarily; so that in respect to essence, and to the clearness and eventual emancipation of spirit, it would be as material a fact as matter ever could be. The question, in cosmology, is not between matter and Ideas but between one sort of matter and another; and it is for experiment and science, not for logic, to discover what sort of matter matter is.

This decisive office of matter remains the same when Souls are introduced into the Platonic cosmology, where they tend to absorb the Ideas and to transpose them into themes or goals of a purely spiritual life.

The transformation is indeed glorious: from being mere essences morally relative to the humblest earthly needs and economy, the Ideas now become This is true spirits shining by their own light, living for of Platonic themselves, and perfectly fulfilling and enjoy- souls. ing their spontaneous destiny. But all this goes on "Yonder", above, in heaven: "Here", to souls awakening and painfully struggling on earth, those celestial spirits remain mere ideals, patrons or models which we may invoke and aspire to imitate; they can be as little affected or moved by us as if they had remained pure essences. Our existence and our vicissitudes are due to an opposite principle. Why, indeed, did a ray from one of those celestial luminaries fructify in this particular lump of clay, and animate me, and not another, with a felt need and an awakening will, aspiring to contemplate and ultimately to possess that, and no other, heavenly perfection? What called down and buried here, in my private animal psyche, a seed and replica of that particular celestial spirit? Evidently, again, some predisposition, readiness, or responsiveness peculiar to my earthly substance. Perhaps, if my nature at birth was not due to my material heritage, and to the accumulated organisation of an endless series of ancestors, it might be attributed, according to a venerable fable, to my own vicissitudes in previous lives. In this case, if my transmigrations had no beginning, my fatal character—or my fatal acts, making irruption from moment to moment into my character—must be among the primary free constituents of the universe. They must be factors, combining with the other original factors, if any, in determining the flux of existence.

We may give these factors a psychological name and call them wills or acts of will; we may even represent them to be conscious, or prophetic of an intended result; and we may thus assimilate Platonism to panpsychism or to the world of literary psychology. But, if the previous argument be cogent, we shall not thereby avoid an ultimate materialism. The foundations of existence cannot in any case be other than existent, temporal, and arbitrary. Even if the conscious universe were plaited together out of the biographies of everlasting souls, dramatically interwoven, the realm of matter would still be their only possible theatre. It would establish their conjunctions, fix their dates, measure their journeys, and impose on them, through their bodies, all their providential adventures. Plato, Plotinus, and the Indians never conceived the thing otherwise: and this material underpinning to the migration of souls seems indeed indispensable, if they are to be supposed to communicate and interact, as is requisite for all the offices of charity. The material world could hardly be denied, so long as philosophy remained frankly and dogmatically religious.

Their migrations and conjunctions occur by incarnation in matter.

The case is changed, however, when we adopt a strict monadology and ascribe the illusion of society to the moral burden of each separate soul, and to its infinite capacity for dreaming. Matter then seems really to vanish from the universe; yet all its blind fertility and mysterious involution has entered into the soul. Whether the spiriting away of materialism in this direction is nominal or real may be discovered by the study of modern idealism.

Modern idealism has been in a great measure rooted in psychologism and identical with it: in that measure I have already indicated the surviving materialism on which it leans. But through the transcendental door the Germans long ago abandoned that uninhabitable mansion; and their national idealism may be said to begin where psychologism ends. What, then, are the relations of this national philosophy to materialism?

In the first place, like Platonism, German idealism seems to elude materialism by systematically sub-

stituting concepts for substances and descriptions of
things for the things themselves.   It moves in the
plane of Ideas and leaves obscure their relation   Modern
to particular passing facts.   Or rather, it re-   idealism
duces this relation to identity: for the choice of   a revision
of Hebrew
concepts and descriptions is no longer dictated   prophecy.
by moral preoccupations, or spiritual wisdom; it is
made in the act of surveying the facts themselves in
the spirit of prophecy.   Its origin is biblical.   Like
the Hebrew prophets, Protestant philosophers tend
to reject the supernatural and to search nature and
history for the divine plan of events.   They are prophets not so much in foretelling the future—though,
by way of warning, they sometimes venture to do so—
as in speaking in the name of the Lord, who is the power
in matter, delivering his judgments and magnifying
his ways.   In contrast to the Platonists, they show
the greatest respect for the flux of existence.   The
Ideas or laws which they proclaim and regard as powers
are simply tropes supposed to be discernable in that
flux.   This discernment is inevitably personal and
relative; for obviously a moving world, where divisions
are as fluid as positions, is rebellious to any specific
essence, even to fixed patterns or laws of change.
There may be a dialectic inherent in certain attitudes:
but how often does any mind or any revolution obey
it?   The flux of actual existence is untamably complex,
and the tropes visible to the prophet will almost inevitably repeat the outlines of his religious or national
passions, his private insights, or his fine pleasure in
the inner complications of logic or mathematics.   His
prophecy or history, seen from a distance, will seem
only to have added, by its own novelty, one more to
the multitude of unharnessable facts.

But let me suppose that he escapes this fatality, and
traces, for once, perhaps in the person of Hegel, the
exact essence realised in the flux of existence.   The Idea,

or master-trope, enshrined in his system, will then be a true summary of all truth. But truth is eternal:

The prophecy could not be true unless matter conspired to realise it progressively.

neither as a whole nor in any of its parts is it an existence, but only a description of existence. Granting, then, that the truth had been revealed to the prophetic idealist and that he had described existence, on the whole, as it actually is, this existence would still, for that very reason, remain outside of his mind and of his description. A description could not be true, or superior as knowledge to any rival description, if things of their own accord and in their own persons had not independently exemplified that description and rendered the assertion of it true. Thus if any descriptive idealism were true, its very truth would imply and posit the natural world, which is the realm of matter, existing in itself, and justifying that description.

I believe that many who call themselves idealists take this for granted and have never doubted the substantial existence of nature and society diffused about them. If they protest that materialism is absurd and exploded, they do so only because by matter they understand some pictorial or mathematical idol substituted for the pregnant and unfathomable substance of things; and they would disown their own idealism no less decisively, as a rhetorical idol in its turn, if they understood it to deny the scattered and measurable existence of the natural world.

There are, however, a few masters of idealism who

Pure idealism, if it admits truth or belief at all, relapses into psychologism.

despise such a crude philosophy and insist that descriptions are the only knowable facts and descriptive only of their own essence. Being and knowing, they say, are nothing but thinking, and knowledge grows by closer inspection of consciousness, not by information coming from outside or referring to anything ulterior.

Very well: this at least is a radical position; yet if we take it consistently we renounce that claim to truth in our ideas which had originally recommended idealism to the innocent believer. We are abolishing the very notion of truth; and if we retain any system of nature or history, we retain it only as a fashionable mode of thought, a fading dream for the moment entertaining the spirit. Even this pleasing assurance about ourselves, that we may create, survive, and develop our absolute experiences, would forsake us unless we still asserted, with a desperate inconsistency, the transcendent validity of memory and expectation: an assertion which reverts to the belief in truth, and restores psychologism, if not humanism, with all its materialistic implications. We cannot, in fact, outgrow materialism without outgrowing belief altogether. And unless I am much mistaken, it is restiveness under belief of any sort, because it is precarious and a check, while it lasts, on spontaneous life, that has inspired all modern or Protestant philosophy. The assertion of a new belief, contradicting the old, is only a feint in the battle against all dogma. The new belief would prove no less odious, and probably far more absurd, than the old, were it ever seriously established; but its very weakness is a recommendation to a spirit unwilling to be pledged, detesting to be taught, and wedded to nothing but the romantic sport of imposing and deriding its successive illusions. All parties, all ages, Hegel tells us, are mad; yet the folly of all the parts secretly vindicates the rationality of the whole, since every part destroys itself because of its irrationality.

Heraclitus of old had said something of the same sort; but that freer and wiser man was not deceived, or bound to deceive others, concerning the principle of this universal instability. It was fire, it was matter: and what, indeed, is this barbarous self-ignorance and self-treason save

Vague will is the expression of matter ill organised.

the voice of matter, profoundly rebellious to form, and incapable of existing except in the act of leaping from one form to another? Matter, to blind feeling, is but force without, and will within. It seems everywhere instinct with life; yet life and will are not really possible without a modicum of material organisation, stable enough to give foothold and some specific direction to the tentative actions and conquests destined to enlarge it. The paths of life are many, and most of them without issue. Knowledge of nature and of self, in clarifying the blind materialism of action, enlightens this choice of direction, proves it to have been fruitful, and enables it still to be so. The steady habit of matter within, in the psyche, meets and feeds on its steady variations without; and life attains the dignity of the rational animal. Without this definition in character and this recognition of matter, life can only grope and flounder, vehemently agitated by a vague wretchedness, without either courage to confess its limits or lucidity to see its goal.

It is therefore by no means necessary that some satirical critic should point out the fundamental

Idealism materialism of these idealists; it is plainly
transformed confessed by their own aspirations. There
into panthe- is nothing for which they manifest a greater
istic sym-
pathy with contempt than for the merely ideal; they are
existence intent on reality. Reason, Life, and Ideas, when by definition existent and creative, evidently forfeit their original moral values: for they are no longer essentially fulfilments and perfections desired by that which exists, but its actual nature or cause. They have become, like matter, the primal accident; and this fact is far from lowering them in the estimation of the modern enthusiast. The passion at work in his bosom is the will to live; his idealism expresses his vitality, not any squeamish requirements about the conditions of existence or any sure promises concerning

its issue. Why should a few knocks, or a great many holocausts, chill his ardour in living in God's world? His ancestors hardly required a touch of sardonic piety to be edified by the prospect of almost universal damnation. He may well brace himself in his turn to face the same fatality spread thin, and distributed impartially throughout the writhings of history. And if moral judgment is jeopardised or quite surrendered in this brave optimism, moral sentiment still remains; because the happy adventurer is now convinced that in accepting the universe as it is, and appropriating as much of it as possible, he is partaking in the divine life more and more abundantly.

I have said that the Ideas distinguished by Platonists were for the most part ideals never realised in this world; they were the sort of tropes interesting to moralists and poets, and essentially forms of the good. But in modern idealism Ideas are meant to be descriptions of the actual course of nature and history: they are alleged laws. *In pantheism physics has the whip hand.* Now the laws of nature are important in considering the means to an end, but they are not ends nor relevant to the choice of ends. For a Platonist a world governed by natural laws—that is, obeying the habits which it once has formed—would be formless, since its form would not be relevant to the good. It could not become a form of the good until a life arising under those material auspices began to look to it as to a condition of its happiness. In many modern Idealists a dose of this Platonism is mixed with their pantheistic and optimistic ethics, but only to the confusion of thought; for when a sentimentalist becomes a historian, or in self-defence a natural philosopher, he insensibly falsifies the facts and laws which actually hold, in order to insinuate others which have an edifying rather than a descriptive value. Yet it is as little philosophical to beautify reality as to be afraid of it. The face of existence, as open to an omnivorously curious mind, is sublime and fascinating enough, but it is surely more than human, less than moral, other than dialectical. It is something like the universe of Spinoza, which even if stretched a little by his dogmatic logic and idealised by his traditional piety, is essentially the natural world, the realm of matter. This certainly embodies some essence—Spinoza thought it embodied all essences—but the only ideal toward which it moves is that all things shall become what in eternity they are; that nature shall run its course, that every appointed event shall occupy its allotted place, and that opinions shall supersede one another as they do, by a psychological and economic necessity: and this is precisely the picture of the universe painted by modern idealists, when they are strong-minded. Their idealism adds nothing to Spinoza on the ideal side, rather subtracts: but it adds a transcendental preface showing that this picture is the work of thought, as if that improved it.

This pantheism, being Hebraic in origin, sees reality in time rather than in space, and is historical rather than cosmological; and being modern, it approaches reality through the discovery or experience of it, and is fundamentally subjective. But there is no moral idealism left in it, unless it is by making the upshot of history as flattering as possible to local or human interests; in other words, by misrepresenting the truth. This is not to say that pantheism is irreligious; on the contrary, there is a sense in which moral idealism, since it selects, protests, and aspires, is less religious than the unqualified worship of reality. When the heart is bent on the truth, when prudence and the love of prosperity dominate the will, science must insensibly supplant divination, and reverence must be transferred from traditional sanctities to the naked power at work in nature, sanctioning worldly

Respect for matter is the beginning of wisdom.

wisdom and hygienic virtue rather than the maxims of
zealots or the dreams of saints. God then becomes
a poetic symbol for the maternal tenderness and the
paternal strictness of this wonderful world; the ways
of God become the subject-matter of physics. Matter,
the principle of genesis and the true arbiter of fortune,
has often been one of the realities symbolised under
the name of God, as truth has often been another; and
nothing is more normal than that the magnetism of
surrounding substance, with its thousand assaults and
its thousand responses, should exercise a sobering
guidance over the human soul. As the mere rigidity
and grimace of a stock or stone can bring primitive
man to his knees, annihilating his waywardness by
the relentless authority of its stark Being, so the discovered march of nature in its treacherous fecundity
can hypnotise the philosopher, and cause him to disown
as impious his hopeless private idealisms. It is now
his only idealism to be humble, to be wise, to be content with his finitude. This form of religion is more
materialistic than materialism, since it assigns to
matter a dignity which no profane materialist would
assign to it, that of having *moral* authority over the
hearts of men.

Yet in some measure matter deserves respect even
in the eyes of the Platonist, whose aspiration seems
at first sight to be to escape from it; for It is requi-
goodness is a prerogative which matter may site for a full
acquire, as it acquires beauty, in so far as it harmony
falls into living organisms and feeds their intelligence
capacity for intuition and feeling with an and truth.
abundance of kindred things. The avowed materialist
also, who professes to be an intelligent animal, cannot
but place a part of his happiness in his understanding
of the world. It is easier to change one's pleasures
than to change the nature of things. Why not adapt
these passionate demands of ours — so vague and

helpless beyond the circle of our domestic needs—to that larger economy by which we must live, if we are to live at all? The study of nature and the equalising blows of experience tend to establish this sort of regenerate and disillusioned piety in the place of the arrogant idealisms of the will. Human utopias begin to seem childish in the face of the facts, and the facts, in their labyrinthine order and polyglot fertility, end by seeming glorious as well as inevitable. There are always compensations for the brave, even in death; and a part of the soul rejoices and becomes immortal in its sympathies when it countersigns the death-warrant of all the other parts.

This fundamental materialism in all human wisdom leaves the spirit perfectly free to exercise its originality in the sphere of poetry and feeling; but it shows that in so far as spirit takes the form of intelligence and of the love of truth (which is also an ideal passion of the soul) it must assume the presence of an alien universe and must humbly explore its ways, bowing to the strong wind of mutation, the better to endure and to profit by that prevailing stress. It was in the act of making this assumption that animal sensibility first became intelligence. In its further explorations, spirit discovers, as far as it is possible or needful, its urgent and compulsory objects, as well as the organs, ailing or healthful, which give it play. Finally, with this self-knowledge, spirit completes its round and renders its philosophy secure and its ambitions spiritual: for it has now conceived how it came into existence and how it is the natural light by which existence, in its waking moments, understands itself.

INDEX

Action, posits the field for physics, 9 ; excludes doubt, 9 ; distinguishes fact from fancy, 21 ; moves in a relative cosmos, 21-22
Animal faith, the basis of physics, 3, 6
Apollo, a symbol for intuition, 32 ; for light, 45
Aristotle, 20, 87, 138, 141, 153, 170
Art, requires prior organisation, 129 ; extends the range of the psyche, 160 ; implies benefit, 161
Association of ideas, 173
Atomic theory, its generic truth, 39
Atoms, pictorial units, 38 ; contigent, 39 ; not existing as defined, 40, 82

Before and after, organic relations, 93
Behaviour, the object of scientific psychology, 123, 153, 154
Berkeley, 168-171

Change, not an illusion, 75, 76 ; not internal to intuitions, 79 ; how represented there, 80, 81
Chaos, fundamental, 99 ; would be re-established by a sincere psychologism, 173
Consciousness, cf. *Spirit*
Contingency, may be incidental, 110 ; permeates facts and laws, 113, 114
Continuity, inseparable from change, 81
Copernicus, 7

Dante, 54, 55
Democritus, viii, 19, 40, 98
Derivation, necessary to successiveness, 16

Descartes, viii, 20, 40, 165
Dionysus, 31
Dog and the bone, 28, 29
Duration, 63, 80

Einstein, 7 ; his theory adumbrated, 96
Eleatic influence in physics, 19
Empiricism, its relative justification, 111
Epicurus, 1
Essences, not causes, 84 ; nor complete facts, 86
Evolution, cf. *Flux*
Existence, how felt, 9 ; a passage from potentiality to act, 93
External relations, defined, 14 ; necessary to existence, 11-13

Final causes exist, 119, 120 ; but only in moral retrospect, 127, 131, 134, 135 ; mystification regarding them, 193, 194
Flux, a corollary to contingency, 14 ; essential to substance, 15, 16 ; excludes synthesis, 77 ; requires matter, 99 ; fertile in everything possible, 133-135
Food, intrinsic function of substance, 92
Free-will, either accident, 195 ; or expression of a formed nature, 196
Freud, 31

Genesis, the book of, 7 ; of moments, 89

Hegel, 199, 201
Henry VI, 129
Heredity, insecure, 126
History, philosophies of, 3
Homer, 95

THE END